THE AMERICAN CIVIL WAR

Other books in the
Opposing Viewpoints in World History series:

OPPOSING VIEWPOINTS®
IN WORLD HISTORY

THE AMERICAN CIVIL WAR

Wim Coleman and Pat Perrin,
Book Editors

Bruce Glassman, *Vice President*
Bonnie Szumski, *Publisher*
Helen Cothran, *Managing Editor*

**OPPOSING
VIEWPOINTS®
SERIES**

GREENHAVEN PRESS
An imprint of Thomson Gale, a part of The Thomson Corporation

Detroit • New York • San Francisco • San Diego • New Haven, Conn.
Waterville, Maine • London • Munich

3 4633 00196 2446

LIBRARY OF CONGRESS CATALOGING-IN-PUBLICATION DATA

The American Civil War / Wim Coleman and Pat Perrin, book editors.
    p. cm. — (Opposing viewpoints in world history series)
Includes bibliographical references and index.
ISBN 0-7377-2019-0 (lib. : alk. paper) — ISBN 0-7377-2020-4 (pbk. : alk. paper)
    1. United States—History—Civil War, 1861–1865. 2. United States—History—
Civil War, 1861–1865—Sources. I. Coleman, Wim. II. Perrin, Pat. III. Series.
E468.A53 2005
973.7—dc22   2004047349

Printed in the United States of America

✸ Contents

was rampant in the prewar North. The goal of ending slavery has probably been exaggerated as the Union's motive for waging war.

Chapter 2: Were the Actions of the North Legal and Moral?

Chapter 4: What Is the Legacy of the Civil War?

✸ Foreword

On December 2, 1859, several hundred soldiers gathered at the outskirts of Charles Town, Virginia, to carry out, and provide security for, the execution of a shabbily dressed old man with a beard that hung to his chest. The execution of John Brown quickly became and has remained one of those pivotal historical events that are immersed in controversy. Some of Brown's contemporaries claimed that he was a religious fanatic who deserved to be executed for murder. Others claimed Brown was a heroic and selfless martyr whose execution was a tragedy. Historians have continued to debate which picture of Brown is closest to the truth.

The wildly diverging opinions on Brown arise from fundamental disputes involving slavery and race. In 1859 the United States was becoming increasingly polarized over the issue of slavery. Brown believed in both the necessity of violence to end slavery and in the full political and social equality of the races. This made him part of the radical fringe even in the North. Brown's conviction and execution stemmed from his role in leading twenty-one white and black followers to attack and occupy a federal weapons arsenal in Harpers Ferry, Virginia. Brown had hoped to ignite a large slave uprising. However, the raid begun on October 16, 1859, failed to draw support from local slaves; after less than thirty-six hours, Brown's forces were overrun by federal and local troops. Brown was wounded and captured, and ten of his followers were killed.

Brown's raid—and its intent to arm slaves and foment insurrection—was shocking to the South and much of the North. An editorial in the *Patriot*, an Albany, Georgia, newspaper, stated that Brown was a "notorious old thief and murderer" who deserved to be hanged. Many southerners expressed fears that Brown's actions were part of a broader northern conspiracy against the South—fears that seemed to be confirmed by captured letters documenting Brown's ties with some prominent northern abolitionists, some of whom had provided him with financial support. Such alarms also found confirmation in the pronouncements of some speakers such as writer Henry David Thoreau, who asserted that

Brown had "a perfect right to interfere by force with the slave-holder, in order to rescue the slave." But not all in the North defended Brown's actions. Abraham Lincoln and William Seward, leading politicians of the nascent Republican Party, both denounced Brown's raid. Abolitionists, including William Lloyd Garrison, called Brown's adventure "misguided, wild, and apparently insane." They were afraid Brown had done serious damage to the abolitionist cause.

Today, though all agree that Brown's ideas on racial equality are no longer radical, historical opinion remains divided on just what Brown thought he could accomplish with his raid, or even whether he was fully sane. Historian Russell Banks argues that even today opinions of Brown tend to split along racial lines. African Americans tend to view him as a hero, Banks argues, while whites are more likely to judge him mad. "And it's for the same reason—because he was a white man who was willing to sacrifice his life to liberate Black Americans. The very thing that makes him seem mad to white Americans is what makes him seem heroic to Black Americans."

The controversy over John Brown's life and death remind readers that history is replete with debate and controversy. Not only have major historical developments frequently been marked by fierce debates as they happened, but historians examining the same events in retrospect have often come to opposite conclusions about their causes, effects, and significance. By featuring both contemporaneous and retrospective disputes over historical events in a pro/con format, the Opposing Viewpoints in World History series can help readers gain a deeper understanding of important historical issues, see how historical judgments unfold, and develop critical thinking skills. Each article is preceded by a concise summary of its main ideas and information about the author. An in-depth book introduction and prefaces to each chapter provide background and context. An annotated table of contents and index help readers quickly locate material of interest. Each book also features an extensive bibliography for further research, questions designed to spark discussion and promote close reading and critical thinking, and a chronology of events.

✪ Introduction

It is now well over a century after the end of the Civil War. Many issues that were fiercely argued during the war remain as hotly debated as ever, with no resolution in sight. Perhaps this is because students of the war demand "either/or" answers. Insisting on one answer or another may indicate a failure to understand the Civil War as a process, always changing and evolving—not only in the past, but to the present day. A look at three debates central to the Civil War—whether it was fought about secession or emancipation, whether a Confederate defeat was inevitable, and whether the Union was worth preserving—reveals the difficulty of grasping the Civil War with either/or answers. "There are trivial truths and the great truths," observed the physicist Niels Bohr. "The opposite of a trivial truth is plainly false. The opposite of a great truth is also true."[1] The Civil War seems to be a fascinating wellspring of opposing great truths.

Secession or Emancipation?

Some historians insist that the Civil War was fought over the issue of secession; the South was determined to preserve its liberty and independence, while the North was equally determined to preserve the Union. Other historians insist that the war was fought over the issue of slavery; the South was determined to keep its "peculiar institution," while the North was equally determined to end it. The fierceness of the debate between these viewpoints suggests that only one or the other can be true. But viewing the war as a process reveals truth in both arguments.

The war certainly had roots in American slavery. As the nineteenth century progressed, slavery flourished throughout the South, and abolitionist sentiment grew throughout the North. Abolitionists were especially adamant that slavery not expand westward. In 1854 the Republican Party was founded largely to oppose slavery's expansion—indeed, its very existence. The South became increasingly bitter about Northern agitation over slavery.

In November 1860, Republican candidate Abraham Lincoln was

11

elected president of the United States. Lincoln was notorious in the South for his "A House Divided" speech of June 16, 1858, in which he had asserted, "I believe this government cannot endure, permanently half *slave* and half *free*."[2] Lincoln's election was the last straw for the South. Starting with South Carolina, states began seceding before Lincoln even took office, citing the threat to the institution of slavery as their principal reason. Moreover, the Confederate Constitution, adopted on March 11, 1861, assured slavery's continuance:

> In all such territory [added to the Confederacy] the institution of negro slavery, as it now exists in the Confederate States, shall be recognized and protected by Congress and by the Territorial government; and the inhabitants of the several Confederate States and Territories shall have the right to take to such Territory any slaves lawfully held by them in any of the States or Territories of the Confederate States.[3]

Thus the election of an antislavery president provoked the secession of a region deeply committed to slavery. By the time of Lincoln's inauguration on March 4, 1861, seven states had seceded, and the divided Union teetered on the brink of war. Six weeks after the inauguration, Confederate guns fired on the federal Fort Sumter in Charleston, South Carolina, and the war began. To some abolitionists—notably the brilliant escaped slave Frederick Douglass—the conflict was an "abolition war" from the very outset. Observing the war's beginnings from England, the German-born political philosopher Karl Marx thought so as well.

But Lincoln himself said otherwise. In his first inaugural address, delivered before the war's onset, Lincoln assured the South that he had no desire to interfere with the institution of slavery. The man who had eloquently denounced slavery suddenly seemed not to care about emancipation. Secession was another matter. Lincoln considered the Union inviolable, and preserving it was his only stated reason that war might become necessary. This turnaround puzzled and disturbed some of Lincoln's contemporaries. It troubles and disturbs Americans today—and helps convince some historians that emancipation was never a true issue of the war.

To demonstrate Lincoln's supposed indifference to the cause of emancipation, Lincoln's critics often quote his famous letter to the *New York Tribune*'s editor Horace Greeley, dated August 22, 1862:

> My paramount object in this struggle *is* to save the Union, and is *not* either to save or to destroy slavery. If I could save the Union without freeing *any* slave I would do it, and if I could save it by freeing *all* the slaves I would do it; and if I could save it by freeing some and leaving others alone I would also do that. What I do about slavery, and the colored race, I do because I believe it helps to save the Union; and what I forbear, I forbear because I do *not* believe it would help to save the Union. I shall do *less* whenever I shall believe what I am doing hurts the cause, and I shall do *more* whenever I shall believe doing more will help the cause.

Critics claim that Lincoln here damns himself with his own words; the so-called Great Emancipator was a hypocrite who did not care about emancipation except out of political expediency. However, this letter is typically quoted selectively, omitting Lincoln's crucial last two sentences:

> I shall try to correct errors when shown to be errors; and I shall adopt new views so fast as they shall appear to be true views.
>
> I have here stated my purpose according to my view of *official* duty; and I intend no modification of my oft-expressed *personal* wish that all men every where could be free.[4]

Lincoln ends by qualifying all he has said before—and by acknowledging the constantly evolving nature of the war.

Indeed, Lincoln's Emancipation Proclamation of January 1, 1863, made emancipation a reason for the fighting. Lincoln was painfully aware of the proclamation's limitations; as a wartime commander in chief, he could proclaim the freedom of slaves only in areas under Confederate control. He therefore vigorously promoted the passage of the Thirteenth Amendment to formally end American slavery. Although Lincoln did not live to see the amendment's ratification on December 6, 1865, he witnessed its approval by Congress in January of that year. In his second inaugural address of March 4, 1865, Lincoln seemed to flatly contradict his earlier sentiments, saying, "All knew that this interest [slavery] was, somehow, the cause of the war."[5]

So, Lincoln's motives for waging war were not static and simple but dynamic and complex. He also had a Bohr-like capacity to embrace seemingly opposite truths. He came to consider the Union and emancipation not as separate issues but as somehow identical. As the great source of the possibilities for democracy, the Union must be preserved; as a massive obstacle to democracy, slavery must be destroyed. It is not really a contradiction that Lincoln's first inaugural address was concerned with the Union while his second inaugural address was concerned with emancipation. To Lincoln, the two goals were deeply connected but always shifting in importance, one predominant over the other by turns.

Sentiments of ordinary Americans regarding the war were equally complicated. For instance, it is true that many Union soldiers believed they had enlisted in a war against secession and bitterly resented the Emancipation Proclamation. They had no desire to die for the freedom of a supposedly inferior race. It is equally true that Union soldiers wrote and zealously sang variants of "The John Brown Song," honoring the famous abolitionist outlaw. Many Union soldiers became fervent abolitionists themselves upon marching south and witnessing the depredations of slavery. One can grasp this paradox by viewing the war (as Lincoln himself did) as evolving. Over time, the war was fought about *both* secession and emancipation.

Doomed or Victorious?

In addition to arguments over the cause of the war, debate continues over the outcome of the conflict—whether the Confederacy's defeat was inevitable from the start or whether the South at least stood a chance of victory. In a way, this debate leads to a deeper paradox than the debate over whether the war was fought over secession or slavery. For it is possible that a clear-cut victory has yet to be won by either the Union or the Confederacy even today.

In many ways, the Confederacy was enormously outgunned and outmanned. The Union dwarfed the Confederacy in sheer size. Twenty-three states remained in the Union, while only eleven seceded. Some 21 million people lived in Union states, while only

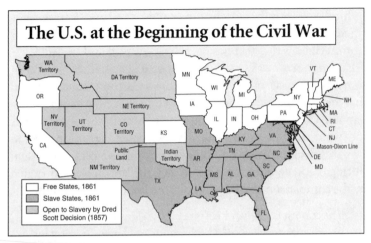

about 9 million lived in the Confederacy, about 3.5 million of whom were African American slaves. Thus the Union had many more eligible fighting men. Northern soldiers outnumbered Confederate soldiers by about four to one. Moreover, Union manufacturing was almost six times that of the largely agricultural Confederacy, giving Northern military forces staggering superiority in everything from uniforms to munitions to telegraph lines to railroads. Indeed, after the firing on Fort Sumter, a quick Union victory seemed inevitable. As the poet Walt Whitman recalled after the war,

> Nine-tenths of the people of the free States look'd upon the rebellion, as started in South Carolina, from a feeling one-half of contempt, and the other half composed of anger and incredulity. . . . A great and cautious national official predicted it would blow over "in sixty days," and folks generally believ'd the prediction. . . . I remember, too, that a couple of companies of the Thirteenth Brooklyn, who rendezvou'd at the city armory, and started thence as thirty days' men, were all provided with pieces of rope, conspicuously tied to their musket-barrels, with which to bring back each man a prisoner from the audacious South, to be led in a noose, on our men's early and triumphant return![6]

However, the Union's overconfidence evaporated after the First Battle of Bull Run on July 21, 1861, a decisive Confederate victory.

In hindsight, Southern defeat may appear to have been predestined; during the war itself, however, the outcome seemed far from certain as the fortunes of each side waxed and waned.

Union morale was low during the first stages of the war. Even some abolitionists, notably William Lloyd Garrison, initially argued that the Confederacy should be allowed to go its way in peace. Perhaps the Confederacy did not need military victories to preserve its independence. All it had to do was wear down the Union's will to fight, much as the American colonies had done against Great Britain during the Revolutionary War. In fact, the British were intrigued by the comparison. As the editors of the London *Times* put it,

> The contest is really for empire on the side of the North, and for independence on that of the South, and in this respect we recognize an exact analogy between the North and the Government of George III, and the South and the Thirteen Revolted Provinces.[7]

The British government kept a keen eye on the conflict, its interests and sympathies largely with the Confederacy. After Confederate general Robert E. Lee's triumph at the Second Battle of Bull Run in August 1862, the British were all but ready to come to the Confederacy's aid, much as France had done for the American colonies during the Revolutionary War. British involvement certainly would have affected the progress of the war.

But on September 17, 1862—the bloodiest single day in American history—the South suffered a wrenching defeat at Antietam. The British thought twice about intervening. Lincoln seized the rare victory to issue his preliminary Emancipation Proclamation of September 22, followed by the full Emancipation Proclamation of January 1, 1863. Once the Union war effort turned into a crusade against slavery, Britain considered it wise to maintain neutrality.

It might be argued that a Confederate victory at Antietam, followed by British intervention, would have assured a Southern victory. Or perhaps the war would have ended differently if Robert E. Lee had won the Battle of Gettysburg, crushing the Union's morale by successfully invading Pennsylvania in the summer of 1863. Given these scenarios, one might even imagine the Confederate States of America maintaining its independence to the present day.

Interestingly, such possibilities typically have been most heatedly denied by many Confederate sympathizers, who maintain that the South could have prolonged the war but could never have won it. The always inevitable defeat became imminent when Ulysses S. Grant assumed command of Union forces in 1864. No chivalrous, gentlemanly warrior (at least in Southern eyes), Grant simply overwhelmed the South with staggering manpower and matériel. And when Grant unleashed General William Tecumseh Sherman to rip a sixty-mile-wide path of destruction across Georgia in late 1864, the South was utterly finished.

Proponents of this "Lost Cause" retelling of the Civil War prefer to call the conflict the War Between the States, the War of Southern Secession, the War of Southern Independence, or the War of Northern Aggression. According to the Lost Cause view, the Confederacy was the tragic underdog in a brutally unjust war. The South fought not for the perpetuation of slavery but for the preservation of states' rights and the survival of its quaint, agrarian culture against heartless, industrialized Northern invaders.

The Lost Cause view has permeated popular culture in song and story, especially in novels such as Margaret Mitchell's Pulitzer Prize–winning *Gone with the Wind* and movies such as D.W. Griffith's 1915 epic *Birth of a Nation*. It has gained remarkable credence in both the North and South, and throughout the rest of the United States. According to some recent historians, wide acceptance of the Lost Cause view has led to a kind of Confederate victory, a *propaganda* victory that allowed some of the worst aspects of Southern life to continue for decades after the war. As historian David Brion Davis put it, writing in 2001,

> The United States is only now beginning to recover from the Confederacy's ideological victory following the Civil War. Though the South lost the battles, for more than a century it attained its goal: that the role of slavery in America's history be thoroughly diminished, even somehow removed as a cause of the war.[8]

Not surprisingly, Lost Cause proponents argue with equal vehemence that historians like Davis have themselves hijacked history during the last half century. They claim that such historians

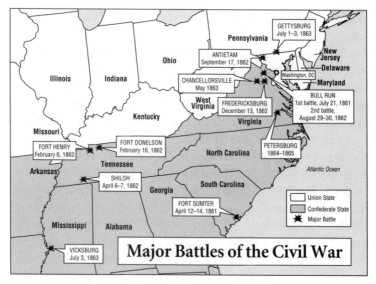

Major Battles of the Civil War

have unduly praised barbaric Union military leaders like Grant and Sherman; have made a martyred hero out of Lincoln, whom they consider a power-mad dictator; have exaggerated the importance of slavery to the Confederate cause; and have committed a host of other crimes against historical fact.

The Civil War, it seems, continues—not on battlefields but in the world of ideas. To be sure, Civil War reenactors perform a valuable service in portraying the gritty feel of what battlefields were really like. But reenactors are, after all, only pretending. To witness the Civil War still raging in earnest, one need only turn to historical journals, hundreds of books on the topic published every year, or a multitude of Internet Web sites and discussion boards. As it did during the four years before Lee's surrender at Appomattox, the war keeps changing, unfolding, and evolving even today.

Union: Blessing or Curse?

After the war, the Union was preserved, but at the cost of hundreds of thousands of American lives and the destruction of the Southern way of life. Historians sometimes question whether the Union was worth such a sacrifice. Some regard the Union as a positive good, others as a pernicious evil. This controversy seems timeless, for it reflects on the past, present, and future of American government.

Some historians argue that the United States was not even a nation when the Civil War broke out but merely a loosely linked network of allied sovereign states. Although the Constitution strengthened the federal government, state and local governments largely looked after themselves through the early part of the nineteenth century. True, during the years preceding the Civil War, the telegraph, railroads, and increasingly sophisticated printing presses made distances seem smaller, and the rise of big business helped knit different parts of the United States together economically. But it is debatable whether these developments enhanced the country's national feeling or served instead to highlight differences between regions.

After the Confederacy's defeat, the Union assumed what might be described as revolutionary powers. As historian Garry Wills puts it,

> Up to the Civil War, "the United States" was invariably a plural noun: "The United States are a free government." After Gettysburg, it became a singular: "The United States is a free government." This was the result of the whole mode of thinking Lincoln expressed in his acts as well as his words, making *union* not a mystical hope but a constitutional reality.[9]

Thus the United States after the Civil War was founded on the basis of a more profound concept of Union than had existed before.

Lincoln himself insisted that the Union was nothing new or revolutionary. In his first inaugural address, he argued that it predated even the United States. The Union, he said, was formed by the Articles of Association in 1774—two years before independence was declared. The Declaration of Independence strengthened this Union. America's first constitution, the Articles of Confederation of 1778, cemented it further by proclaiming "perpetual union," one of Lincoln's favorite phrases. The Constitution of 1787 rendered the Union truly perpetual, claiming as one of its objects "to form a more perfect Union."

Lincoln believed that an indissoluble Union was the great hope for the unfulfilled promise of American democracy, what he called (echoing the Declaration of Independence) "the proposition that all men are created equal."[10] This philosophy was put to work immediately after the war, when the Republican-controlled federal government went to work on the issue of racial equality. In 1865 the Thirteenth Amendment to the Constitution abolished slavery. The Civil Rights Act of 1866 assured the basic rights of citizens to African Americans. In 1868 and 1870, respectively, the Fourteenth and Fifteenth amendments guaranteed further rights to African Americans, including the right to vote. Finally came the Civil Rights Act of 1875, which ruled against most kinds of segregation. While all these measures were being enacted, federally led postwar Reconstruction sought not merely to bring Southern states back into the Union but to undo the effects of hundreds of years of slavery.

When Reconstruction ended in 1877, the Southern states defied postwar civil rights laws and amendments with Jim Crow laws enforcing racial segregation and essentially reducing African Americans in the South to a status little better than slavery. This situation continued until the 1950s, when the federal government again began to intervene. In 1954 the Supreme Court declared public school segregation unconstitutional. Congress passed the twentieth century's first civil rights bills in 1957 and 1960. Far more effective were the Civil Rights Act of 1964 and the Voting Rights Act of 1965.

Today's liberal thinkers sometimes cite this history as affirmation of Lincoln's belief in the democratic nature of a federal Union. In their view, strong central government has been necessary to keep states from denying rights to minorities. For at times, minorities must be protected from what legal scholar Lani Guinier (echoing the Constitution's principal framer, James Madison) has called "the tyranny of the majority."[11]

By no means did all of Lincoln's contemporaries agree with his interpretation of American history; not all historians agree with it today. Some contend that the Union as it exists today was not created in 1774, 1776, 1778, or 1787, but was, as Wills suggests, largely created by Lincoln during the Civil War.

In contrast to liberals, conservatives typically take a dimmer view of this expansion of the federal government's role. In their view, the notion of a centralized, monolithic government serving the cause of freedom and democracy defies common sense. Particularly odious to most conservatives are forced busing in order to desegregate schools and affirmative action policies to ensure employment for minorities and women. Federal financial assistance programs, including welfare, Social Security, Medicaid, and Medicare, also come under conservative criticism.

This attitude is strikingly consistent with the long-defunct Confederate Constitution. Closely modeled on the U.S. Constitution, the Confederate Constitution nevertheless tellingly omits the phrase "promote the general Welfare" from its preamble. The Confederacy was founded on the belief that centralized government had a minimal role to play in people's lives; "the general Welfare" was best left to states, local governments, or the people themselves. Many of today's conservatives agree with this un-Lincolnian, anti-Union view of democratic government.

Thus today's divisions between "liberal" and "conservative" largely began when the concept of Union was so profoundly transformed during the Civil War. Instead of waning over the years, these divisions arguably have deepened. Indeed, they may be deepening every day. The military phase of the Civil War ended in 1865, but the ideological war continues.

The Civil War Today

Recent years have brought heated controversy concerning whether the Confederate battle flag should be flown above Southern public buildings, especially state capitols. At a glance, this may seem a trivial issue. But the emotions it touches run deep. Opponents of the battle flag—especially people of color—consider it as a symbol of hatred and racism not unlike the Nazi swastika. Proponents of the flag regard it as a symbol of patriotism and bravery in defense of one's homeland. The controversy hints at deeper divisions still, divisions in political thought and in people's dreams and hopes for American society. Lincoln's appeal in his second inaugural address "to finish the work we are in; to bind up the nation's wounds"[12] seems disturbingly relevant today.

The celebrated historian Bruce Catton once wrote the following about the Civil War:

With its lights and its shadows, its rights and its wrongs, its heroic highlights and its tragic overtones—it was not an ending but a beginning. It was not something that we painfully worked our way to, but something from which we made a fresh start. It opened an era instead of closing one; and it left us, finally, not with something completed, but with a bit of unfinished business which is of very lively concern today and which will continue to be of lively concern after all of us have been gathered to our fathers.[13]

Catton wrote these words in 1958, in the midst of the civil rights movement. He might as well have written them today, since divisions dating back to the Civil War continue to trouble the nation. For the sake of our nation's present and future, Americans must continue to try to understand the Civil War and its legacy—and to view the war itself as continuing to change and evolve before our eyes. It is simply not over. "The past is never dead," observed that great chronicler of Southern life William Faulkner. "It's not even past."[14]

Notes

1. Niels Bohr, *New York Times*, October 20, 1957.
2. Abraham Lincoln, "A House Divided" speech, Springfield, Illinois, June 16, 1858.
3. Constitution of the Confederate States of America, March 11, 1861.
4. Abraham Lincoln, letter to Horace Greeley, August 22, 1862.
5. Abraham Lincoln, second inaugural address, March 4, 1865.
6. Walt Whitman, *Specimen Days*, 1875.
7. *Times* (London), November 7, 1861.
8. David Brion Davis, "The Enduring Legacy of the South's Civil War Victory," *New York Times*, August 26, 2001.
9. Garry Wills, *Lincoln at Gettysburg: The Words That Remade America.* New York: Simon & Schuster, 1992, p. 145.
10. Abraham Lincoln, Gettysburg Address, November 19, 1863.
11. Lani Guinier, *Tyranny of the Majority: Fundamental Fairness Is Representative Democracy.* New York: Simon & Schuster, 1995, p. 3.
12. Lincoln, second inaugural address.
13. Bruce Catton, *America Goes to War: The Civil War and Its Meaning in American Culture.* Hanover, NH: Wesleyan University Press, 1958, p. 12.
14. William Faulkner, *Requiem for a Nun.* New York: Vintage, 1975, p. 80.

CHAPTER 1

What Were the Causes of the Civil War?

⊛ Chapter Preface

Without secession, there would have been no Civil War. Secession was not a new concept when South Carolina broke from the Union on December 20, 1860. Indeed, to secession's proponents, the idea seemed as old as the Declaration of Independence and its affirmation of people's right "to alter or to abolish" forms of government that fail to suit their interests. On the other hand, antisecessionists believed that the United States' founding documents made the Union inviolable and secession unlawful.

Secession was debated during the early years of the American republic. The New England states briefly considered seceding in 1814. But as the United States grew increasingly polarized over slavery, secession became specifically a Southern issue. The threat of Southern secession was temporarily quelled by the Missouri Compromise of 1820, which admitted Missouri as a slave state and carefully divided western territories into free and slave areas.

Then came the nullification crisis of 1832. Statesman John C. Calhoun, following arguments originated by Thomas Jefferson and James Madison, proposed that the sovereignty of states allowed them to nullify federal laws. Calhoun's theory led his native state of South Carolina to the brink of secession. President Andrew Jackson, anticipating Lincoln's later advocacy of the Union, stated his opposition to secession:

> The Constitution of the United States . . . forms a *government*, not a league; and whether it be formed by compact between the states or in any other manner, its character is the same. It is a government in which all the people are represented, which operates directly on the people individually, not upon the states; they retained all the power they did not grant. But each state, having expressly parted with so many powers as to constitute, jointly with the other states, a single nation, cannot, from that period, possess any right to secede, because such secession does not break a league but destroys the unity of a nation; and any injury to that unity is not only a breach

which would result from the contravention of a compact but it is an offense against the whole Union.[1]

Lacking support from other Southern states, South Carolina did not secede during the nullification crisis. But threats of Southern secession mounted during the 1840s and 1850s.

The 1848 victory in the Mexican War added vast western territories to the United States. Debate over whether these territories should become free or slave led the Union yet again to the brink of dissolution. The Compromise of 1850, which admitted California as a free state and left the question of slavery up to the governments of Utah and New Mexico, temporarily defused the crisis. But the compromise also contained the seeds of future problems. It included a Fugitive Slave Act, which forced citizens in free states to return escaped slaves to their owners. This law increased abolitionist sentiment in free states and deepened the divide between North and South.

In a further attempt to hold the Union together through compromise, Senator Stephen A. Douglas sponsored the Kansas-Nebraska Act of 1854. As the Compromise of 1850 had done for Utah and New Mexico, the Kansas-Nebraska Act made slavery in the territories a matter of popular sovereignty; that is, the decision of whether their territories should be free or slave was left to the people of Kansas and Nebraska. This act was bitterly denounced by Douglas's political rival Abraham Lincoln, and popular sovereignty led to violence in Kansas between pro- and antislavery factions. The Kansas-Nebraska Act also spurred the creation of the Republican Party, which dedicated itself to stopping the expansion of slavery.

The 1860 election of Republican presidential candidate Abraham Lincoln provoked the long-threatened secession of South Carolina. Other Southern states, perceiving a threat to the institution of slavery—and to their very way of life—followed in quick succession. Lincoln had not even taken office before six other states seceded and the Confederate States of America had been formed. Lame-duck Democratic president James Buchanan regarded secession as illegal but believed that force could not be used to restore the Union.

In his first inaugural address of March 4, 1861, Abraham Lincoln echoed Andrew Jackson's 1832 argument that states had no right to secede. He warned that America teetered on the brink of war and implored the rebellious states to return to the Union peacefully. But on April 12, 1861, Southern guns fired on federal Fort Sumter in Charleston, South Carolina. In a July 4 message to Congress, Lincoln placed the responsibility for the war squarely on the rebellious states' shoulders:

> Then, and thereby, the assailants of the Government, began the conflict of arms, without a gun in sight, or in expectancy, to return their fire, save only the few in the Fort, sent to that harbor, years before, for their own protection, and still ready to give that protection, in whatever was lawful. In this act, discarding all else, they have forced upon the country, the distinct issue: "Immediate dissolution, or blood."[2]

Lincoln then asked for congressional assistance in what he expected to be "a short, and a decisive" conflict.

Viewpoints in this chapter debate whether secession was legal, whether restoring the Union was a desirable goal, and whether Northern aggression was justified. The final two viewpoints focus on slavery and the role it played in dividing the Union and instigating the war.

Notes

1. Andrew Jackson, proclamation to the people of South Carolina, December 10, 1832.
2. Abraham Lincoln, message to Congress in special session, July 4, 1861.

Viewpoint 1

"If disunion must come, let it come without war."

The Northern States Should Let the Southern States Secede

Albany Atlas and Argus

After the Southern states began to secede, the lame-duck Democratic president, James Buchanan, declared himself powerless to stop the rebellion, despite his belief that secession was illegal. Kentucky senator John J. Crittenden proposed compromises designed to restore the Union; these would have included constitutional amendments assuring the Southern states of the continuation of slavery. Once the Crittenden Compromise was defeated, war seemed to be the only remaining means of recovering the original Union.

The Democratic newspaper *Albany Atlas and Argus* had supported Stephen A. Douglas in the election of 1860, warning that Lincoln's election would lead to secession. In the following viewpoint, written after four states had seceded, the newspaper's editors rank themselves among the "thinking men" who foresaw this division. Now that secession has occurred, the editors argue that the South should be allowed to go its way in peace.

Albany Atlas and Argus, editorial, January 12, 1861.

The sectional doctrines of the Republican party have—as think-ing men have foreseen—at last brought us to the verge of civil war. Indeed, war has already commenced. Four States have for-mally separated from the Confederacy [Union] and declared them-selves independent of the Federal Union and are in the attitude of supporting their position by arms. The Republican leaders adhere to their partisan and sectional dogmas and utterly refuse to do any-thing to arrest this impending danger and restore peace to the country. The present Congress will do nothing and before its term expires on the 4th of March, thirteen or fourteen of the slave States will have established a separate government, which they will sus-tain at the hazard of fortune and life. We shall be confronted with the stern issue of peaceable, voluntary separation, or of civil war. We shall be compelled to bid a sad farewell to the brethren with whom we have so long dwelt in liberty and happiness and divide with them the inheritance of our fathers—or to undertake, by all the terrors and horrors of war, to compel them to continue in union with us. We must separate from them peaceably, and each seek happiness and prosperity in our own way—or we must con-quer them and hold them as subjugated provinces. Fellow citizens, of all parties and of whatever past views, which course do you pre-fer? Shall it be peaceable separation or civil war?

Terror and Desolation

If such be the issue—and none can now deny it—before choos-ing war, it will be well to reflect whether it will effect the desired object of preserving the Union of these States? With thirteen or fourteen States banded together and fighting with as much perti-nacity, as our fathers of the Thirteen Colonies, for what *they* deem their rights and liberties, the war must be a deadly and protracted one. We do not doubt that the superior numbers and resources of the Northern States might prevail. We might defeat them in battle, overrun their country, and capture and sack and burn their cities, and carry terror and desolation, by fire and sword, over their several States. We might ruin the commerce and industry of the country, North and South, sweep the whole land with the be-som of war, and cause the nation to resound with the groans of widows and orphans; all this we might do, and through it all, pos-

The Union Is Dissolved

William Lloyd Garrison was perhaps the most outspoken and prominent abolitionist of his time. Quoted here is a January 1861 article in Garrison's newspaper The Liberator, *in which he argues that the slave states should be allowed to secede in peace. Garrison later changed his mind and supported Lincoln's war efforts.*

The people of the North should recognize the fact that THE UNION IS DISSOLVED, and act accordingly. They should see, in the madness of the South, the hand of God, liberating them from "a covenant with death and an agreement with hell," made in a time of terrible peril, and without a conception of its inevitable consequences, and which has corrupted their morals, poisoned their religion, petrified their humanity as towards the millions in bondage, tarnished their character, harassed their peace, burdened them with taxation, shackled their prosperity, and brought them into abject vassalage. . . .

Now, then, let there be a CONVENTION OF THE FREE STATES called to organize an independent government on free and just principles; and let them say to the slave States—"Though you are without excuse for your treasonable conduct, depart in peace! Though you have laid piratical hands upon property not your own, we surrender it all in the spirit of magnanimity! And if nothing but the possession of the Capitol will appease you, take even that, without a struggle! Let the line be drawn between us where free institutions end and slave institutions begin! Organize your own confederacy, if you will, based on violence, tyranny, and blood, and relieve us from all responsibility for your evil course!"

Wendell Phillips Garrison and Francis Jackson Garrison, *William Lloyd Garrison*, vol. 4. New York: Houghton Mifflin, 1894.

sibly, be able to boast of the triumph of the Federal arms, and to see the stars and stripes wave over every battle field and every smoking city.

But would peace thereby be restored? Would the Union be thus preserved? Would these conquered States quietly assume their old places in the Confederacy? Would they send Representatives to Congress, take part in the Presidential elections, and perform their functions as loyal members of the Union? Would they be anything but conquered States, held in subjection by military restraint? No—peace and concord between these States cannot be reached through the medium of war. The probable result of a long and deadly struggle would be a treaty of peace, agreeing to a division. War is necessarily disunion and division, and we prefer division without war—if it must come. By a peaceable separation the enmities of the two sections will not be inflamed beyond all possible hope of reconciliation and reconstruction, but war will be eternal hostility and division. Let the people of this country pause before they draw the sword and plunge into a fratricidal strife.

Danger of the War Spirit

We say emphatically, let the great State of New York not be foremost in kindling a flame, which never will be quenched except in the blood of our kindred. The public passions are easily aroused and the great danger at this moment is that the war spirit will take possession of the populace and hurry us and the country on to ruin. The press, influential citizens, legislators and other public men—instead of inflaming this feeling and seeking ephemeral popularity by ministering to it, should seek to restrain it and lead the people of this State to act with moderation. New York should not forget her position, as the most powerful State of the Union and should put forth her influence, in this emergency, in favor of peace, and if she cannot stay the mad torrent of disunion, should hold herself in condition to be able, when the passions of men shall have cooled, to engage in the work of reconstruction and of reuniting States now dissevered, for causes so trivial that time and reflection—if we escape war—may be expected to remove them.

We repeat—if disunion must come, let it come without war. Peaceable separation is a great calamity—but dissolution, with the superadded horrors of internal war, including the ruin of business, the destruction of property, oppressive debt, grinding taxation and sacrifice of millions of lives, is a scourge from which, let us pray, that a merciful Providence may protect us.

If the present Congress, and the political leaders in it, who have brought the country into this danger, have not the patriotism to adopt measures for the restoration of peace, better than plunge the nation into civil war, let them propose Constitutional amendments, which will enable the people to pass upon the question of a voluntary and peaceful separation. Then, at least the hope will remain that the people may in good time discard their fanatical political leaders and apply themselves to the reconstruction and renovation of the Constitution and the Union.

Viewpoint 2

"Peaceable separation leads as surely to war as night follows day."

The Northern States Should Not Let the Southern States Secede

Peoria Daily Transcript

Aside from waging war, how could the North resolve the growing secession crisis? One option was to try to lure the rebellious states back into the Union by means of a compromise. Kentucky senator John J. Crittenden attempted to accomplish this goal with a series of measures that included a constitutional amendment protecting slavery. Another option was peaceful separation, a popular course that found support among even such confirmed abolitionists as William Lloyd Garrison. Yet another option was to do nothing; this seemed to be the course chosen by Lincoln's lame-duck Democratic predecessor, President James Buchanan.

In the viewpoint that follows, the editors of the Illinois newspaper *Peoria Daily Transcript* renounce these three options as doomed to failure. The editors insist that there is only one vi-

Peoria Daily Transcript, editorial, February 22, 1861.

able choice: to restore the Union by any means. The South cannot be allowed to willfully commit an illegal act, and the North must be ready to use military force if necessary to secure the Union.

When men get into a difficulty the great question is to get out. The people of the United States are in the midst of a great national difficulty. Let us cast aside the question how we came in it, who is to blame in the matter, and address ourselves to the question how we shall get out. If our dwelling were on fire we would not spend our time running about to ascertain through whose culpability or carelessness it occurred, but we would go at once to work to quell the conflagration.

Several methods have been proposed for the settlement of our national troubles, which we propose now to consider. They are, 1st, Compromise, 2d, Peaceable Separation, 3d, Masterly Inactivity, 4th, Enforcement of the Laws.

The first method, that of compromise in the manner proposed in Congress (amendment to the Constitution of the United States) is, in the present condition of the country, wholly out of the question. We need not discuss whether such a course is proper or improper. It is sufficient that it is impossible. The Constitution of the United States requires the concurrence of three-fourths of the States to give force and vitality to any amendment. To do this, twenty-six States must concur. Seven have left the Union and will not vote. At least a half dozen of the remaining States will vote down any amendment that may be proposed. The border States will vote them down if they do not concede their demands, and certain Northern States will vote them down if they do. Any compromise not incorporated into the Constitution will not be accepted by the South. Any compromise not incorporated into the Constitution in the manner proposed by that instrument will not be accepted by the North. To incorporate amendments in the manner provided we have shown to be impossible, and that puts an end to the first method.

Peaceable separation is proposed by those who perceive that compromise is impolitic or impossible, and who hope by it to avoid war. But peaceable separation leads as surely to war as night follows day. The United States would not allow Great Britain, France, Russia, nor all Europe combined, to maltreat citizens as our citizens are maltreated daily at the South, without war.—Maritime and border disputes would arise which would plunge us into strife before six months had passed over the heads of the two confederacies. Escape of slaves and attempted recapture and reprisals would bring the people to blows without any action of the two governments. We fought Great Britain in 1812 for one-half the provocation that would be given us. No dread of civil war would stay our hands. The Southern Confederacy would be a foreign nation. We would not have to fight it for once only, but unless we absolutely conquered it, we should have to fight it forever. It would be hostile in interests, hostile in institutions, hostile in everything.

The third method is that of "masterly inactivity," the policy inaugurated by our present imbecile executive [President James Buchanan]. Such a course leads to national debasement, anarchy and ruin. It is a confession that no power exists in the government for the enforcement of the laws, or that we are too cowardly to enforce them. Our revenue would be cut off, for if the South refuse to pay duties the North will refuse likewise. We could not raise money by taxation, for we can no more collect taxes than we can collect revenue.

Uphold the Constitution

The fourth method is enforcement of the laws. This is the only method that indicates the least chance of success. People say we have no right to coerce a State. We say a State has no right to contravene the Constitution. The Constitution of the United States, is in certain particulars supreme, and is clothed with full power to enforce those particulars. Every law passed by a State or the people of a State, in contravention of the Constitution is null and void. Any attempt to enforce those pretended laws is without legal sanction, and is as much a crime to be punished as counterfeiting, smuggling, and piracy. The question is,—Is secession right or wrong, lawful or unlawful? If not right and lawful, it ought to be put down. If we attempt to put it down, what are the chances of success? It will be the government against a faction. It will be a nation of seventy years' growth, fighting for the supremacy of the principles which brought it into being, against a wicked combination to defeat those principles. It will be might and right against weakness and wickedness. It will be the memory of the heroes of the revolution, against the dogmas of [South Carolina statesman John C.] Calhoun, the thievings of [Confederate politician and general John B.] Floyd, and perjuries of those who plotted to overturn the Constitution while their oaths to support it were yet warm on their lips. It will be a people with a navy against a people without a navy. It will be a people with the sympathy of the civilized world in its favor, against a people without that sympathy. It will be a people connected by treaties with other governments, against a people cut off from all communication with the rest of mankind. It will be numbers against numbers as four to one, and that one hampered by a servile population ready, it knows not how soon, to rise and cut its throat. It will be wealth ready to be poured into the lap of the Government, against oppressive taxation and forced loans. It will be all the holy traditions, treasured songs, brave speeches and glories of the past, the Declaration of Independence, the love of freedom, the hopes of the future, the preservation of free speech and a free press, against the eruption of a plague spot, and the rebellion of a petty oligarchy who would "rather reign in hell than serve in Heaven." Under these circumstances who doubts our success? We have the right and the might, and there is no such word as fail.

Viewpoint 3

"The constitutional compact has been deliberately broken and disregarded by the nonslaveholding states; and . . . South Carolina is released from her obligation."

Secession Is Justified

South Carolina Convention

When Abraham Lincoln was elected president in November 1860 with no electoral votes at all from south of the Mason-Dixon Line, South Carolina's state legislature immediately called for a special convention. On December 20, 1860, by a unanimous convention vote, South Carolina became the first state to secede from the Union. Lincoln had not yet taken office as president.

The following viewpoint is the convention's declaration of secession, which painstakingly echoes the words and ideas of the Declaration of Independence, the U.S. Constitution, and even the 1783 Treaty of Paris that ended the Revolutionary War. South Carolina wanted to make abundantly clear that secession was legal—that, indeed, the state was maintaining the traditions of the American Revolution and the Constitution. Among reasons for secession, the declaration emphasizes the activities of abolitionists, the refusal of Northern states to enforce fugitive slave laws, and the election of an antislavery president. Contrary to the arguments of many historians, a perceived threat to slavery clearly was an important cause of Southern secession.

Frank Moore, ed., *The Rebellion Record: A Diary of American Events, with Documents, Narratives, Illustrative Incidents, Poetry, etc., etc.* New York: G.P. Putnam, 1864.

The people of the state of South Carolina, in convention assembled, on the 2nd day of April, A.D. 1852, declared that the frequent violations of the Constitution of the United States by the federal government, and its encroachments upon the reserved rights of the states, fully justified this state in their withdrawal from the federal Union; but in deference to the opinions and wishes of the other slaveholding states, she forbore at that time to exercise this right. Since that time, these encroachments have continued to increase, and further forbearance ceases to be a virtue.

And, now, the state of South Carolina, having resumed her separate and equal place among nations, deems it due to herself, to the remaining United States of America, and to the nations of the world, that she should declare the immediate causes which have led to this act.

The Right of Self-Government

In the year 1765, that portion of the British empire embracing Great Britain undertook to make laws for the government of that portion composed of the thirteen American colonies. A struggle for the right of self-government ensued, which resulted, on the 4th of July, 1776, in a Declaration, by the colonies, "that they are, and of right ought to be, *free and independent states;* and that, as free and independent states, they have full power to levy war, conclude peace, contract alliances, establish commerce, and to do all other acts and things which independent states may of right do."

They further solemnly declared that whenever any "form of government becomes destructive of the ends for which it was established, it is the right of the people to alter or abolish it, and to institute a new government." Deeming the government of Great Britain to have become destructive of these ends, they declared that the colonies "are absolved from all allegiance to the British Crown, and that all political connection between them and the state of Great Britain is, and ought to be, totally dissolved."

In pursuance of this Declaration of Independence, each of the thirteen states proceeded to exercise its separate sovereignty; adopted for itself a constitution, and appointed officers for the administration of government in all its departments—Legislative, Executive, and Judicial. For purposes of defense, they united their arms and their counsels, and, in 1778, they entered into a league known as the Articles of Confederation, whereby they agreed to entrust the administration of their external relations to a common agent, known as the Congress of the United States, expressly declaring, in the 1st Article, "that each state retains its sovereignty, freedom, and independence, and every power, jurisdiction, and right which is not, by this Confederation, expressly delegated to the United States in Congress assembled."

The Treaty with Great Britain

Under this Confederation, the War of the Revolution was carried on; and on the 3rd of September, 1783, the contest ended, and a definite treaty was signed by Great Britain, in which she acknowledged the independence of the colonies in the following terms:

> Article I. His Britannic Majesty acknowledges the said United States, viz.: New Hampshire, Massachusetts Bay, Rhode Island and Providence Plantations, Connecticut, New York, New Jersey, Pennsylvania, Delaware, Maryland, Virginia, North Carolina, South Carolina, and Georgia, to be *free, sovereign, and independent states;* that he treats with them as such; and, for himself, his heirs, and successors, relinquishes all claims to the government, propriety, and territorial rights of the same and every part thereof.

Thus were established the two great principles asserted by the colonies, namely, the right of a state to govern itself; and the right of a people to abolish a government when it becomes destructive of the ends for which it was instituted. And concurrent with the establishment of these principles was the fact that each colony became and was recognized by the mother country as a *free, sovereign, and independent state.*

The Constitution

In 1787, deputies were appointed by the states to revise the Articles of Confederation; and on September 17, 1787, these deputies recommended, for the adoption of the states, the Articles of Union, known as the Constitution of the United States.

The parties to whom this Constitution was submitted were the several sovereign states; they were to agree or disagree, and when nine of them agreed, the compact was to take effect among those concurring; and the general government, as the common agent, was then to be invested with their authority.

If only nine of the thirteen states had concurred, the other four would have remained as they then were—separate, sovereign states, independent of any of the provisions of the Constitution. In fact, two of the states did not accede to the Constitution until long after it had gone into operation among the other eleven; and during that interval, they each exercised the functions of an independent nation.

By this Constitution, certain duties were imposed upon the several states, and the exercise of certain of their powers was restrained, which necessarily impelled their continued existence as sovereign states. But, to remove all doubt, an amendment was added which declared that the powers not delegated to the United States by the Constitution, nor prohibited by it to the states, are reserved to the states respectively, or to the people. On the 23rd of May, 1788, South Carolina, by a convention of her people, passed an ordinance assenting to this Constitution, and afterward altered her own constitution to conform herself to the obligations she had undertaken.

The Law of Compact

Thus was established, by compact between the states, a government with defined objects and powers, limited to the express words of the grant. This limitation left the whole remaining mass of power subject to the clause reserving it to the states or the people, and rendered unnecessary any specification of reserved rights. We hold that the government thus established is subject to the two great principles asserted in the Declaration of Independence; and we hold further that the mode of its formation subjects it to a third fundamental principle, namely, the law of compact. We maintain that in every compact between two or more parties, the obligation is mutual; that the failure of one of the contracting parties to perform a material part of the agreement entirely releases the obligation of the other; and that, where no arbiter is provided, each party is remitted to his own judgment to determine the fact of failure, with all its consequences.

In the present case, the fact is established with certainty. We assert that fourteen of the states have deliberately refused for years past to fulfill their constitutional obligations, and we refer to their own statutes for the proof.

The Fugitive Slave Provision

The Constitution of the United States, in its 4th Article, provides as follows: "No person held to service or labor in one state, under the laws thereof, escaping into another shall, in consequence of any law or regulation therein, be discharged from such service or labor, but shall be delivered up, on claim of the party to whom such service or labor may be due."

This stipulation was so material to the compact that without it that compact would not have been made. The greater number of the contracting parties held slaves, and they had previously evinced their estimate of the value of such a stipulation by making it a condition in the ordinance for the government of the territory ceded by Virginia, which obligations, and the laws of the general government, have ceased to effect the objects of the Constitution. The states of Maine, New Hampshire, Vermont, Massachusetts, Connecticut, Rhode Island, New York, Pennsylvania, Illinois, Indiana, Michigan, Wisconsin, and Iowa have enacted laws which either nullify the acts of Congress or render useless any attempt to execute them. In many of these states the fugitive is discharged from the service of labor claimed, and in none of them has the state government complied with the stipulation made in the Constitution.

Antislavery Feeling

The state of New Jersey, at an early day, passed a law in conformity with her constitutional obligation; but the current of antislavery feeling has led her more recently to enact laws which render inoperative the remedies provided by her own laws and by the laws of Congress. In the state of New York even the right of transit for a slave has been denied by her tribunals; and the states of Ohio and Iowa have refused to surrender to justice fugitives charged with murder and with inciting servile insurrection in the state of Virginia. Thus the constitutional compact has been deliberately broken and disregarded by the nonslaveholding states; and the consequence follows that South Carolina is released from her obligation.

The ends for which this Constitution was framed are declared by itself to be "to form a more perfect union, to establish justice, insure domestic tranquillity, provide for the common defense, promote the general welfare, and secure the blessings of liberty to ourselves and our posterity." These ends it endeavored to accomplish by a federal government in which each state was recognized as an equal and had separate control over its own institutions. The right of property in slaves was recognized by giving to free persons distinct political rights; by giving them the right to represent, and burdening them with direct taxes for, three-fifths of their slaves; by authorizing the importation of slaves for twenty years; and by stipulating for the rendition of fugitives from labor.

Abolitionist Agitation

We affirm that these ends for which this government was instituted have been defeated, and the government itself has been destructive of them by the action of the nonslaveholding states. Those states have assumed the right of deciding upon the propriety of our domestic institutions; and have denied the rights of property established in fifteen of the states and recognized by the Constitution. They have denounced as sinful the institution of slavery; they have permitted the open establishment among them of societies, whose avowed object is to disturb the peace of and eloign the property of the citizens of other states. They have encouraged and assisted thousands of our slaves to leave their homes; and, those who remain, have been incited by emissaries, books, and pictures to servile insurrection.

For twenty-five years this agitation has been steadily increasing, until it has now secured to its aid the power of the common government. Observing the *forms* of the Constitution, a sectional party has found, within that article establishing the Executive Department, the means of subverting the Constitution itself. A geographical line has been drawn across the Union, and all the states north of that line have united in the election of a man to the high office of President of the United States whose opinions and purposes are hostile to slavery. He is to be entrusted with the administration of the common government, because he has declared that "Government cannot endure permanently half slave, half free," and that the public mind must rest in the belief that slavery is in the course of ultimate extinction.

This sectional combination for the subversion of the Constitution has been aided, in some of the states, by elevating to citizenship persons who, by the supreme law of the land, are incapable of becoming citizens; and their votes have been used to inaugurate a new policy, hostile to the South and destructive of its peace and safety.

The Union Dissolved

On the 4th of March next this party will take possession of the government. It has announced that the South shall be excluded from the common territory, that the judicial tribunal shall be made sectional, and that a war must be waged against slavery until it shall cease throughout the United States.

The guarantees of the Constitution will then no longer exist; the equal rights of the states will be lost. The slaveholding states will no longer have the power of self-government or self-protection, and the federal government will have become their enemy.

Sectional interest and animosity will deepen the irritation; and all hope of remedy is rendered vain by the fact that the public opinion at the North has invested a great political error with the sanctions of a more erroneous religious belief.

We, therefore, the people of South Carolina, by our delegates in convention assembled, appealing to the Supreme Judge of the world for the rectitude of our intentions, have solemnly declared that the Union heretofore existing between this state and the other states of North America is dissolved; and that the state of South Carolina has resumed her position among the nations of the world, as [a] separate and independent state, with full power to levy war, conclude peace, contract alliances, establish commerce, and to do all other acts and things which independent states may of right do.

Viewpoint 4

"No state, upon its own mere motion, can lawfully get out of the Union."

Secession Is Not Justified

Abraham Lincoln

By the time Abraham Lincoln was inaugurated as president on March 4, 1861, his election had provoked seven states to secede from the Union—South Carolina, Mississippi, Florida, Alabama, Georgia, Louisiana, and Texas. On February 4, those states had formed the Confederate States of America, with Jefferson Davis as president. When Lincoln took his oath of office, the states of Virginia, North Carolina, Maryland, Kentucky, Missouri, and Tennessee were debating whether to join the Confederacy.

When Lincoln made his first inaugural address, reprinted as the following viewpoint, he was faced with secession and the threat of civil war. His concern was the Union, not slavery. The impassioned "Great Emancipator" of the later Gettysburg Address and the second inaugural address is not to be found here.

Lincoln assures rebellious Southerners that he will not interfere with slavery, that he will uphold fugitive slave laws, and even that he will not object to a proposed constitutional amendment (never passed) to forever protect slavery where it already exists. But secession is another matter. Lincoln argues that the Union is indissoluble and that secession is illegal; therefore, the

Abraham Lincoln, inaugural address, Washington, DC, March 4, 1861.

rebellious states must return peacefully to the Union. The new president's appeal fell on defiant ears. Six weeks after his speech, the Confederacy fired upon Fort Sumter, a federal army post in South Carolina, and the American Civil War began.

F ellow Citizens of the United States:
In compliance with a custom as old as the government it-self, I appear before you to address you briefly and to take, in your presence, the oath prescribed by the Constitution of the United States to be taken by the President "before he enters on the exe-cution of his office."

I do not consider it necessary, at present, for me to discuss those matters of administration about which there is no special anxiety or excitement. Apprehension seems to exist among the people of the Southern states that, by the accession of a Republican admin-istration, their property and their peace and personal security are to be endangered. There has never been any reasonable cause for such apprehension. Indeed, the most ample evidence to the con-trary has all the while existed and been open to their inspection. It is found in nearly all the published speeches of him who now addresses you.

No Intent to Abolish Slavery

I do but quote from one of those speeches when I declare that "I have no purpose, directly or indirectly, to interfere with the insti-tution of slavery in the states where it exists. I believe I have no lawful right to do so, and I have no inclination to do so." Those who nominated and elected me did so with full knowledge that I had made this and many similar declarations, and had never re-canted them. And, more than this, they placed in the platform, for my acceptance, and as a law to themselves and to me, the clear and emphatic resolution which I now read:

> Resolved, that the maintenance inviolate of the rights of the states, and especially the right of each state, to order and con-trol its own domestic institutions according to its own judg-ment exclusively is essential to that balance of power on

which the perfection and endurance of our political fabric depend; and we denounce the lawless invasion by armed force of the soil of any state or territory, no matter under what pretext, as among the gravest of crimes.

I now reiterate these sentiments; and in doing so, I only press upon the public attention the most conclusive evidence, of which the case is susceptible, that the property, peace, and security of no section are to be in any way endangered by the now incoming administration. I add, too, that all the protection which, consistently with the Constitution and the laws, can be given will be cheerfully given to all the states when lawfully demanded, for whatever cause—as cheerfully to one section as to another.

Fugitive Slaves

There is much controversy about the delivering up of fugitives from service or labor. The clause I now read is as plainly written in the Constitution as any other of its provisions:

No person held to service or labor in one state, under the laws thereof, escaping into another, shall, in consequence of any law or regulation therein, be discharged from such service or labor, but shall be delivered up on claim of the party to whom such service or labor may be due.

It is scarcely questioned that this provision was intended by those who made it for the reclaiming of what we call fugitive slaves; and the intention of the lawgiver is the law.

All members of Congress swear their support to the whole Constitution—to this provision as much as to any other. To the proposition, then, that slaves whose cases come within the terms of this clause "shall be delivered up," their oaths are unanimous. Now, if they would make the effort in good temper, could they not, with nearly equal unanimity, frame and pass a law by means of which to keep good that unanimous oath?

There is some difference of opinion whether this clause should be enforced by national or by the state authority; but surely that difference is not a very material one. If the slave is to be surrendered, it can be of but little consequence to him or to others by which authority it is done. And should anyone, in any case, be content that his oath shall go unkept on a merely unsubstantial controversy as to *how* it shall be kept?

Again, in any law upon this subject, ought not all the safeguards of liberty known in civilized and humane jurisprudence to be introduced, so that a freeman be not, in any case, surrendered as a slave? And might it not be well, at the same time, to provide by law for the enforcement of that clause in the Constitution which guarantees that "the citizen of each state shall be entitled to all privileges and immunities of citizens in the several states"?

Disruption of the Union

I take the official oath today with no mental reservations and with no purpose to construe the Constitution or laws by any hypercritical rules. And while I do not choose now to specify particular acts of Congress as proper to be enforced, I do suggest that it will be much safer for all, both in official and private stations, to conform to and abide by all those acts which stand unrepealed than to violate any of them, trusting to find impunity in having them held to be unconstitutional.

It is seventy-two years since the first inauguration of a President under our national Constitution. During that period fifteen different and greatly distinguished citizens have, in succession, administered the executive branch of the government. They have conducted it through many perils, and generally with great success. Yet, with all this scope of precedent, I now enter upon the same task for the brief constitutional term of four years under great and peculiar difficulties.

A disruption of the federal Union, heretofore only menaced, is now formidably attempted.

The Union Is Perpetual

I hold that, in contemplation of universal law and of the Constitution, the Union of these states is perpetual. Perpetuity is implied, if not expressed, in the fundamental law of all national governments. It is safe to assert that no government proper ever had a provision in its organic law for its own termination. Continue to execute all the express provisions of our national Constitution, and the Union will endure forever—it being impossible to destroy it except by some action not provided for in the instrument itself.

Again, if the United States be not a government proper, but an association of states in the nature of contract merely, can it, as a contract, be peaceably unmade by less than all the parties who made it? One party to a contract may violate it—break it, so to speak—but does it not require all to lawfully rescind it? Descending from these general principles, we find the proposition that in legal contemplation, the Union is perpetual, confirmed by the history of the Union itself.

History of the Union

The Union is much older than the Constitution. It was formed, in fact, by the Articles of Association in 1774. It was matured and continued by the Declaration of Independence in 1776. It was further matured, and the faith of all the then thirteen states expressedly plighted and engaged, that it should be perpetual by the Articles of Confederation of 1778. And finally, in 1787, one of the declared objects for ordaining and establishing the Constitution, was "*to form a more perfect Union.*"

But if destruction of the Union by one or by a part only of the states be lawfully possible, the Union is *less* perfect than before the Constitution, having lost the vital element of perpetuity.

It follows from these views that no state, upon its own mere motion, can lawfully get out of the Union—that *resolves* and *ordinances* to that effect are legally void; and that acts of violence within any state or states against the authority of the United States are insurrectionary or revolutionary, according to circumstances.

I therefore consider that, in view of the Constitution and the laws, the Union is unbroken; and to the extent of my ability, I shall take care, as the Constitution itself expressly enjoins upon me, that the laws of the Union be faithfully executed in all the states. Doing this I deem to be only a simple duty on my part; and I shall perform it, so far as practicable, unless my rightful masters, the American people, shall withhold the requisite means or in some authoritative manner direct the contrary.

I trust this will not be regarded as a menace but only as the declared purpose of the Union that it *will* constitutionally defend and maintain itself. In doing this, there needs to be no bloodshed or violence; and there shall be none unless it be forced upon the national authority.

The power confided to me will be used to hold, occupy, and possess the property and places belonging to the government, and to collect the duties and imposts; but beyond what may be necessary for these objects, there will be no invasion—no using of force against or among the people anywhere.

Where hostility to the United States, in any interior locality, shall be so great and universal as to prevent competent resident citizens from holding the federal offices, there will be no attempt to force obnoxious strangers among the people for that object. While the strict legal right may exist in the government to enforce the exercise of these offices, the attempt to do so would be so irritating, and so nearly impracticable withal, that I deem it best to forego, for the time, the uses of such offices.

The mails, unless repelled, will continue to be furnished in all parts of the Union.

So far as possible, the people everywhere shall have that sense of perfect security which is most favorable to calm thought and reflection.

The course here indicated will be followed unless current events and experience shall show a modification or change to be proper; and in every case and exigency, my best discretion will be exercised, according to circumstances actually existing, and with a view and a hope of a peaceful solution of the national troubles, and the restoration of fraternal sympathies and affections.

To Those Who Love the Union

That there are persons in one section or another who seek to destroy the Union at all events and are glad of any pretext to do it, I will neither affirm nor deny; but if there be such, I need address no word to them. To those, however, who really love the Union, may I not speak?

Before entering upon so grave a matter as the destruction of our national fabric, with all its benefits, its memories, and its hopes, would it not be wise to ascertain precisely why we do it? Will you hazard so desperate a step while there is any possibility that any portion of the ills you fly from have no real existence? Will you, while the certain ills you fly to are greater than all the real ones you fly from—will you risk the commission of so fearful a mistake?

All profess to be content in the Union if all constitutional rights can be maintained. Is it true, then, that any right plainly written in the Constitution has been denied? I think not. Happily, the human mind is so constituted that no party can reach to the audacity of doing this. Think, if you can, of a single instance in which a plainly written provision of the Constitution has ever been denied. If, by the mere force of numbers, a majority should deprive a minority of any clearly written constitutional right, it might, in a moral point of view, justify revolution—certainly would, if such right were a vital one. But such is not our case.

Abraham Lincoln

All the vital rights of minorities and of individuals are so plainly assured to them by affirmations and negations, guarantees and prohibitions, in the Constitution that controversies never arise concerning them. But no organic law can ever be framed with a provision specifically applicable to every question which may occur in practical administration. No foresight can anticipate nor any document of reasonable length contain express provisions for all possible questions. Shall fugitives from labor be surrendered by national or by state authority? The Constitution does not expressly say. *May* Congress prohibit slavery in the territories? The Constitution does not expressly say. *Must* Congress protect slavery in the territories? The Constitution does not expressly say.

Secession Is Anarchy

From questions of this class spring all our constitutional controversies, and we divide upon them into majorities and minorities. If the minority will not acquiesce, the majority must, or the government must cease. There is no other alternative; for continuing the government is acquiescence on one side or the other. If a minority, in such case, will secede rather than acquiesce, they make a precedent which in turn will divide and ruin them; for a minority of their own will secede from them whenever a majority refuses to be controlled by such minority.

For instance, why may not any portion of a new confederacy, a year or two hence, arbitrarily secede again, precisely as portions of the present Union now claim to secede from it? All who cherish disunion sentiments are now being educated to the exact temper of doing this. Is there such perfect identity of interests among the states to compose a new Union as to produce harmony only and prevent renewed secession?

Plainly, the central idea of secession is the essence of anarchy. A majority, held in restraint by constitutional checks and limitations, and always changing easily with deliberate changes of popular opinions and sentiments, is the only true sovereign of a free people. Whoever rejects it does of necessity fly to anarchy or to despotism. Unanimity is impossible. The rule of a minority, as a permanent arrangement, is wholly inadmissible; so that, rejecting the majority principle, anarchy or despotism in some form is all that is left.

The Role of the Supreme Court

I do not forget the position assumed by some, that constitutional questions are to be decided by the Supreme Court; nor do I deny that such decisions must be binding in any case upon the parties to a suit as to the object of that suit, while they are also entitled to very high respect and consideration, in all parallel cases, by all other departments of the government. And while it is obviously possible that such decision may be erroneous in any given case, still the evil effect following it, being limited to that particular case, with the chance that it may be overruled and never become a precedent for other cases, can better be borne than could the evils of a different practice.

At the same time, the candid citizen must confess that if the policy of the government, upon vital questions affecting the whole people, is to be irrevocably fixed by decisions of the Supreme Court, the instant they are made, in ordinary litigation between parties in personal actions, the people will have ceased to be their own rulers, having, to that extent, practically resigned their government into the hands of that eminent tribunal.

Nor is there, in this view, any assault upon the Court or the judges. It is a duty from which they may not shrink to decide cases properly brought before them; and it is no fault of theirs if others seek to turn their decisions to political purposes.

One section of our country believes slavery is *right* and ought to be extended, while the other believes it is *wrong* and ought not to be extended. This is the only substantial dispute. The fugitive slave clause of the Constitution and the law for the suppression of the foreign slave trade are each as well enforced, perhaps, as any law can ever be in a community where the moral sense of the people imperfectly supports the law itself. The great body of the people abide by the dry legal obligation in both cases, and a few break over in each. This, I think, cannot be perfectly cured; and it would be worse in both cases *after* the separation of the sections than before. The foreign slave trade, now imperfectly suppressed, would be ultimately revived without restriction in one section; while fugitive slaves, now only partially surrendered, would not be surrendered at all by the other.

We Cannot Separate

Physically speaking, we cannot separate. We cannot remove our respective sections from each other, nor build an impassable wall between them. A husband and wife may be divorced, and go out of the presence and beyond the reach of each other, but the different parts of our country cannot do this. They cannot but remain face to face; and intercourse, either amicable or hostile, must continue between them. Is it possible, then, to make that intercourse more advantageous or more satisfactory *after* separation than *before*? Can aliens make treaties easier than friends can make laws? Can treaties be more faithfully enforced between aliens than laws can among friends? Suppose you go to war, you cannot fight always; and when, after much loss on both sides and no gain on either, you cease fighting, the identical old questions as to terms of intercourse are again upon you.

This country, with its institutions, belongs to the people who inhabit it. Whenever they shall grow weary of the existing government, they can exercise their *constitutional* right of amending it or their *revolutionary* right to dismember or overthrow it. I cannot be ignorant of the fact that many worthy and patriotic citizens are desirous of having the national Constitution amended. While I make no recommendation of amendments, I fully recognize the rightful authority of the people over the whole subject, to be exercised in either of the modes prescribed in the instrument itself; and I should, under existing circumstances, favor rather than oppose a fair opportunity being afforded the people to act upon it.

I will venture to add that, to me, the convention mode seems preferable, in that it allows amendments to originate with the people themselves, instead of only permitting them to take or reject propositions originated by others, not especially chosen for the purpose, and which might not be precisely such as they would wish to either accept or refuse. I understand a proposed amendment to the Constitution—which amendment, however, I have not seen—has passed Congress, to the effect that the federal government shall never interfere with the domestic institutions of the states, including that of persons held to service. To avoid misconstruction of what I have said, I depart from my purpose not to speak of particular amendments so far as to say that, holding such a provision to now be implied constitutional law, I have no objection to its being made express and irrevocable.

Think Calmly and Well

The chief magistrate derives all his authority from the people, and they have conferred none upon him to fix terms for their separation of the states. The people themselves can do this also if they choose; but the executive, as such, has nothing to do with it. His duty is to administer the present government, as it came to his hands, and to transmit it, unimpaired by him, to his successor. Why should there not be a patient confidence in the ultimate justice of the people? Is there any better or equal hope in the world? In our present differences, is either party without faith of being in the right?

If the Almighty Ruler of nations, with His eternal truth and justice, be on your side of the North, or on yours of the South, that truth and that justice will surely prevail, by the judgment of this great tribunal, the American people. By the frame of the government under which we live, this same people have wisely given their public servants but little power for mischief; and have, with equal wisdom, provided for the return of that little to their own hands at very short intervals. While the people retain their virtue and vigilance, no administration, by any extreme of wickedness or folly, can very seriously injure the government in the short space of four years.

My countrymen, one and all, think calmly and *well* upon this whole subject. Nothing valuable can be lost by taking time. If there be an object to *hurry* any of you, in hot haste, to a step which you would never take *deliberately*, that object will be frustrated by taking time; but no good object can be frustrated by it.

Such of you as are now dissatisfied still have the old Constitution unimpaired, and, on the sensitive point, the laws of your own framing under it; while the new administration will have no immediate power, if it would, to change either.

If it were admitted that you who are dissatisfied hold the right side in the dispute, there still is no single good reason for precipitate action. Intelligence, patriotism, Christianity, and a firm reliance on Him, who has never yet forsaken this favored land, are still competent to adjust, in the best way, all our present difficulty.

In *your* hands, my dissatisfied fellow countrymen, and not in *mine* is the momentous issue of civil war. The government will not assail *you*. You can have no conflict without being yourselves the aggressors. *You* have no oath registered in heaven to destroy the government, while *I* shall have the most solemn one to "preserve, protect, and defend" it.

Friends, Not Enemies

I am loathe to close. We are not enemies but friends. We must not be enemies. Though passion may have strained, it must not break our bonds of affection.

The mystic chords of memory, stretching from every battlefield and patriot grave to every living heart and hearthstone all over this broad land, will yet swell the chorus of the Union, when again touched, as surely they will be, by the better angels of our nature.

Viewpoint 5

"Such was the sordid tale of the war which has been called the 'Rebellion,' the 'Civil War' and the 'War Between the States,' but whose real name was the 'War to Preserve Slavery.'"

The Civil War Was a Struggle over Slavery

W.E.B. Du Bois

Born just three years after the end of the Civil War, William Edward Burghardt Du Bois was one of the most influential African American leaders of the first half of the twentieth century. He earned a PhD from Harvard in 1895, cofounded the National Association for the Advancement of Colored People (NAACP) in 1909, and wrote numerous books about the black experience and race relations, including *The Souls of Black Folk* and *The Black Flame.* He also taught history and economics at Atlanta University.

Du Bois was an early black nationalist with socialist leanings whose hopes for racial equality eventually turned to despair. He became especially bitter at how the importance of slavery in causing the Civil War was usually downplayed. In the following viewpoint, written the year before the 1961 Civil War Centennial. Du Bois argues that the war was ultimately a battle over the continuation of slavery in America. A year after writing these words, the elderly and disillusioned Du Bois joined the Com-

W.E.B. Du Bois, "The Lie of History as It Is Taught Today (The Civil War: The War to Preserve Slavery)," *The National Guardian*, February 15, 1960. Copyright © 1960 by *The National Guardian*. Reproduced by permission.

munist Party and moved to Ghana, where he renounced his American citizenship. He died there in 1963.

One hundred years ago next year this nation began a war more horrible than most wars, and all wars stink. From 1861 to 1865 Americans fought Americans, North fought South, brothers fought brothers. All trampled on the faces of four million black folk cowering beneath their feet in mud and blood. Some Americans hated slavery but were unwilling to fight. They would let the "erring sisters depart in peace," with their elegant luxury, cringing service and home-grown concubines. Free Negroes and their white friends organized the escape of slaves and fugitive slaves became a main cause of the war. One man, John Brown, fought slavery with his bare fists and was crucified three years before the flash of Sumter.

So the nation reeled into murder, hate, hurt and destruction until they killed 493,273 human beings in battle, left a million more in pain, and nearly bankrupted the whole nation. "We are not fighting slavery," cried the North. "We are fighting for independence," cried the South. "We are not fighting with Negroes," insisted the North as it returned black fugitives. "Negroes do not want to be free," jeered the South; Negroes whispered: "Let us fight for freedom." The Northerners hated the struggle and nearly all who could bought immunity, while some laborers rioted and hanged Negroes to lamp posts. Most workers refused to volunteer and thousands of soldiers deserted from the ranks.

Outcries from North and South

The South yelled and rushed to war, ran the Northerners home again and again ranted and blundered and tried to frighten victory out of impossible odds, while their soldiers deserted in increasing droves.

Louder and louder rose voices in the North: "Free the slaves!" It was the only real reason for war. Lincoln was firm: "I am not fighting to free slaves but only for Union—union to planting, manufacture and trade." Still voices arose led by Frederick Douglass: "Arm the slaves." Lincoln said: "It would be giving arms to the enemy."

The Northern armies began to use the slaves as servants, stevedores and spies; already the Southerners were using the slaves to guard their families and to raise food and clothes for themselves as they fought the fight for slavery. The world looked in amazement on this new free democracy as it staggered, killed and destroyed, both sides appealing for help.

Slowly in the gloom thousands of black slaves began silently to move from plantation to the camps of the Northern armies. Slowly the nation joined the cry of black and white abolitionists: "Free the slaves!" And the bleeding trenches added: "Arm them. The slaves are already armed with muscles if not with guns. They will feed the slave power unless we use them." Black regiments appeared in Kansas, South Carolina and Louisiana. Finally Lincoln saw the truth and dared to change his mind. He offered compensated emancipation and colonization of blacks abroad: The South refused. The war reached bloody stalemate and the nation trembled. Volunteers ceased to offer and corpses clogged the rivers of Virginia. [Confederate general Robert E.] Lee started North and Lincoln threatened. "Surrender or I abolish slavery," he cried in September 1862, beneath the smoke of Antietam. He armed eventually two hundred thousand slaves and a million awaited his call.

The Negroes Fight

The Negroes fought like the damned, two hundred thousand of them; led by two hundred black officers and subalterns, they tore into a hundred and more battles and left seventy thousand dead and dying on the fields. They served in every arm of service and in every area of struggle. They were slaughtered at Fort Wagner to hold Carolina. They committed suicide at Port Hudson so that the Father of Waters should flow "unvexed to the sea." They were buried in the Crater to help Grant capture Richmond, the capitol of the Confederacy, and a black regiment led Abraham Lincoln through the city singing,

> John Brown's body lies a moldering in the grave
> But his soul goes marching on . . .

The South cursed them and treated them as outlaws: [Confederate general Nathan Bedford] Forrest murdered and burned them at Fort Pillow [Tennessee in April 1864]. But Lincoln testified that without these black soldiers and the hundreds of thousands of Negro laborers, guards, informers and spies we could not have won the war. On January 1, 1863, Lincoln declared the slaves in rebel territory "then, thenceforward and forever free." The South saw hell in the blazing heavens and with one last gasp tried themselves openly to arm the slaves. They failed and Lee surrendered.

The "War to Preserve Slavery"

Such was the sordid tale of the war which has been called the "Rebellion," the "Civil War" and the "War Between the States," but whose real name was the "War to Preserve Slavery." That was the only name which made sense to those who fought the war and those who supported it. It sang in their songs and chanted in their poetry:

> In the beauty of the lilies
> Christ was born across the sea.
> As he died to make men holy,
> Let us die to make men free

Then we turned from the abolition of slavery to our muttons: to making money. Some Americans stepped forward with alms and teachers for the black freed men. Some rushed South to make money with cheap labor and high cotton. But most of the nation tried to forget the Negro. He was free, what more did he want? He asked for a Freedmen's Bureau and got a small one paid for mainly with the unclaimed bounties of dead black soldiers. Philanthropists gave him a bank and cheated him out of most of his savings when it failed. Votes? Nonsense, unless planters demand a lower tariff, payment for the Confederate debt and compensation for freed slaves.

We refused to let the horrible mistake of war teach our children anything. We gave it less and less space in our textbooks, until today slavery gets a paragraph and the Civil War a page.

Moreover, the whole cause and meaning of the war is distorted in 10,000 books which falsify the real story. Now in weighty tome, gaudy magazine and television the war was merely an unfortunate misunderstanding. It seems nobody wanted slavery and the South, having had it forced upon her, was about to abolish it but for senseless, impatient agitation. All of our history from the Missouri Compromise through the Compromise of 1850 to the secession of South Carolina is being thus rewritten and the Negro painted as a contented slave, a lazy freedman, a thieving voter and today as happily integrated into American life.

No Guidance from the Past

Thereupon with no guidance from the past the nation marched on with officers strutting, bands playing and flags flying to secure colonial empire and new cheap slave labor and land monopoly in Asia, Africa and the islands of the seas. We fought two World Wars killing nearly 500,000 American youth, and added 50,000 more dead by "police action" in Korea [1950–1953]. In all we destroyed more wealth than we have since been able to count. We are now wasting $40 billion a year for more wars and we owe $284 billion for past wars. In sixty years we have spent only $14 billion for education.

So now comes the time to celebrate the War to Preserve Slavery. The South, which for a century has insisted that theirs was a just war fought with the highest motives by the noblest of men, is pouring forth books and pamphlets to prove this. This all Southern white children have been taught to believe until it is to most of them a matter of absolute and indisputable truth. Historians, North and South, have spread the story and artists have depicted it, so that most Southern states next year will celebrate as a triumph in human effort this despicable struggle to keep black Americans in slavery.

The North, on the other hand, sees little reason to remember or celebrate this war. It would prefer to forget it, but most Northern states will stage some sort of celebration to recall the keeping of this nation united for producing more millionaires than any other people and for proving what philanthropists we are. We gave and are still giving alms to Negroes.

The South will preen itself. What a courageous folk, lynching singlehanded since the Civil War 5,000 helpless Negroes and disfranchising millions. Virginia will lead the rejoicing with a $1,750,000 centennial budget and Mississippi is following with $500,000.

Arkansas will join in with [segregationist Governor Orval] Faubus, and Georgia will sing the Jubilee, but not with "Marching Through Georgia." Colored citizens will be asked to attest how loyally they protected old master's family while he fought for slavery.

The whole United States will stage a mighty pageant to cost at

Karl Marx's View from England

The German political philosopher Karl Marx, who was living in England during the time of the American Civil War, was one of the keenest Old World observers of the conflict. In the following excerpt from an 1861 article, written almost a year before Lincoln issued his preliminary Emancipation Proclamation, Marx shows an almost prescient conviction that the Civil War is, indeed, about slavery.

The question of the principle of the American Civil War is answered by the battle slogan with which the South broke the peace. [Alexander] Stephens, the Vice-President of the Southern Confederacy, declared in the Secession Congress that what essentially distinguished the Constitution newly hatched at Montgomery from the Constitution of Washington and Jefferson was that now for the first time slavery was recognised as an institution good in itself, and as the foundation of the whole state edifice, whereas the revolutionary fathers, men steeped in the prejudices of the eighteenth century, had treated slavery as an evil imported from England and to be eliminated in the course of time. Another matador of the South, Mr. [Leonidas W.] Spratt, cried out: "For us it is a question of founding a great slave republic." If, therefore, it was indeed only in defence of the Union that the North drew the sword, had not the South already declared that the continuance of slavery was no longer compatible with the continuance of the Union?

Karl Marx, "The North American Civil War," *Die Presse*, no. 293, October 25, 1861.

first $200,000 and millions later. Big Business, including the Stock Exchange and travel bureaus, will play a major part, but the emancipation of slaves will be ignored. So says the head of the Centennial committee, a nice old white gentleman with a black mammy who serves under an army general, called deservedly the Third Ulysses S. Grant.

Leaders and Dreams

Listen America! Hear that we will not celebrate the freeing of four million slaves! O dark Potomac where looms the gloom of the Lincoln Memorial. Father Abraham, unlimber those great limbs; let the bronze blaze with blood and the eyes of sorrow again see. Stand and summon out of the past the woman [Julia Ward Beecher] whose eyes saw "the glory of the coming of the Lord"; the Seer [Ralph Waldo Emerson] who said: "For what avail the plough or sail or land or life if freedom fail?" The abolitionist [William Lloyd Garrison] who cried: "I will not retreat a single inch and I will be heard!" Arouse [Wendell] Phillips and [Charles] Sumner, [Thaddeus] Stevens and [James G.] Birney and the whole legion who hated slavery and let them march to Capitol Hill. Warn them again, that this nation must have a "new birth of freedom" even if "all the wealth piled up by the bondsmen's two hundred and fifty years of unrequited toil shall be sunk" and if "every drop of blood drawn by the lash, be paid by another drawn by the sword." As was said three thousand years ago, so still it must be said that "the judgments of the Lord are true and righteous altogether."

This is but the raving of an old man who has long dreamed that American Negroes could be men and look white America in the face without blinking. Not only dreamed but saw in 1913 the Negroes of six states celebrate the Jubilee of Emancipation without apology. Here in New York we inaugurated an abolition celebration securing a state appropriation of $10,000 and a Negro Board of Control. We spent the money honestly and effectively and centered it on recalling the part which Negroes played in the war. We pictured the progress of American Negroes and the forgotten history of their motherland, Africa. For a week beginning October 21, 1913, in the 11th Regiment Armory, Ninth Avenue and 62nd Street, 30,000 persons attended the celebration and 350 actors took part. Few who saw ever forgot the Egyptian Temple, the Migration of the Bantu and the March of the Black Soldiers. Three times later in Washington, Philadelphia and Los Angeles the pageant was repeated. James Weldon Johnson and I went further and planned for 1918 a Jubilee of the 14th Amendment, but the First World War killed that dream.

The Failure of History

Today no Negro leader who holds a good government appointment, or is favored of the great benevolent foundations or has a job in Big Business, or is financed by the State Department to travel abroad, will dare dream of celebrating in any way the role which Negroes played in the Civil War. It would be "racist" for an "integrated" Negro American to recall the Emancipation of black slaves in the United States. And any Negro school or college would risk its income if it staged a celebration.

Possibly the main moral of all this is the failure of history as it is taught today even to attempt to tell the exact truth or learn it. Rather, so many historians conceive it their duty to teach as truth what they or those who pay their salaries believe ought to have been true. Thus we train generations of men who do not know the past, or believe a false picture of the past, to have no trustworthy guide for living and to stumble doggedly on, through mistake after mistake, to fatal ends. Our history becomes "lies agreed upon" and stark ignorance guides our future.

Viewpoint 6

"The idea that racially enlightened Northerners marched south and died by the hundreds of thousands for the benefit of black strangers . . . and then marched happily back . . . is simply not credible."

Slavery Was Only One Among Many Causes of the War

Thomas J. DiLorenzo

An economics professor at Loyola College in Baltimore, Thomas J. DiLorenzo writes extensively about current events and American history. He is the author of *The Real Lincoln: A New Look at Abraham Lincoln, His Agenda, and an Unnecessary War*, a book in which he takes a decidedly dim view of America's sixteenth president and the Civil War.

In DiLorenzo's view, Lincoln was a ruthless dictator who deliberately destroyed the American founders' dream of a loose federation of states devoted to individual liberty. Lincoln replaced that original plan with a vast, centralized government that usurps the nation's freedoms to this day. In waging and winning his "unnecessary war," Lincoln fulfilled his dark purpose of building an American empire. In the following view-

Thomas J. DiLorenzo, "The Great Centralizer: Abraham Lincoln and the War Between the States," *The Independent Review*, vol. 3, Fall 1998. Copyright © 1998 by the Independent Institute, 100 Swan Way, Oakland, CA 94021-1428 USA. www.independent.org. Reproduced by permission.

point, excerpted from an article for *The Independent Review*, DiLorenzo cites Lincoln's racial comments, the ineffectiveness of the Emancipation Proclamation, and the North's harsh treatment of African Americans to suggest that the abolition of slavery has been exaggerated as a cause of the Civil War.

Historical research on the causes of the War between the States ranges from claims that slavery was the predominant cause to the view of James Ford Rhodes that "of the American Civil War it may safely be asserted that there was a single cause, slavery." Slavery was certainly an important element, but its importance seems to have been exaggerated as much as other causes—particularly economic motivations—have been overlooked or ignored. . . .

Open-minded Americans should consider that many of Lincoln's personal views on race relations can be described only as the views of a white supremacist. Indeed, he even used the words "superior and inferior" to define the "proper" places of the two races in American society. In the September 18, 1858, debate with Senator Stephen Douglas, he stated:

> I will say then that I am not, nor ever have been in favor of bringing about in any way the social and political equality of the white and black races—that I am not nor ever have been in favor of making voters or jurors of Negroes, nor of qualifying them to hold office, nor to intermarry with white people; and I will say in addition to this that there is a physical difference between the white and black races which I believe will for ever forbid the two races from living together on terms of social and political equality. And inasmuch as they cannot so live, while they do remain together there must be the position of superior and inferior, and I as much as any other man am in favor of having the superior position assigned to the white race.

Support for Colonization

When asked what should be done if the slaves were ever freed, Lincoln's initial response was to suggest sending them all back to

Africa: "Send them to Liberia, to their own native land. But free them and make them politically and socially our equals? My own feelings will not admit this." As president, Lincoln held a meeting in the White House with freed black leaders, whom he encouraged to lead a colonization effort back to Africa by example. He developed plans to send freed blacks to Haiti and Central America—anywhere but the United States.

Lincoln's idol [the American statesman] Henry Clay [1777–1852] was a lifelong member of the American Colonization Society and was its president when he died. In his 1852 eulogy, Lincoln approvingly quoted Clay's statement that "there is a moral fitness in the idea of returning to Africa her children." Clay's colonization proposal "was made twenty-five years ago," Lincoln observed, but "every succeeding year has added strength to the hope of its realization.—May it indeed be realized!"

Some ten years later, in his December 1, 1862, message to Congress, Lincoln reiterated that "I cannot make it better known than it already is, that I strongly favor colonization."

No Intention to Disturb Slavery

Lincoln frequently castigated the abolitionists as zealots who "would shiver into fragments the Union of these States; tear to tatters its now venerated constitution; and even burn the last copy of the Bible, rather than slavery should continue a single hour." But being the master politician, he adopted the position of his political role model, slave owner Henry Clay. As described by [historian] Robert Johannsen, that position was "opposition to slavery in principle, toleration of it in practice, and a vigorous hostility toward the abolition movement."

Lincoln had no intention to disturb Southern slavery in 1860. In his First Inaugural Address he announced that "I have no purpose, directly or indirectly, to interfere with the institution of slavery in the States where it exists. I believe I have no lawful right to do so, and I have no inclination to do so." He also promised in the same address to uphold and strengthen the fugitive slave clause of the Constitution, even though lax or nonenforcement of that clause would have quickened slavery's demise. . . .

Lincoln's Emancipation Proclamation did not free a single slave.

The proclamation applied only to rebel territory, even though at the time the North controlled large parts of the South, including much of Tennessee and Virginia, where it would have been possible to emancipate thousands of slaves.

Indeed, many slaves who ended up in the hands of the Union army were not set free but were put to work doing some of the most unpleasant tasks in and around army encampments. Others were sent back to their owners by federal troops.

Congress passed several "confiscation acts," which permitted Union soldiers to confiscate the slaves (and other property) in conquered rebel territory. The slaves were then enslaved by the Union army. As one Illinois lieutenant reported, "I have 11 Negroes in my company now. They do every particle of the dirty work. Two women among them do the washing for the company."

Specifically exempted from the Emancipation Proclamation were the Louisiana parishes of "St. Bernard, Plaquemines, Jefferson, St. John, St. Charles, St. James, Ascension, Assumption, Terrebonne, Lafourche, St. Mary, St. Martin, and Orleans." Also exempted by name were the federally controlled areas of West Virginia, large parts of Virginia, and all the Union-controlled border states, such as Maryland and Kentucky.

A Public Relations Strategy

The *New York World* newspaper sharply criticized Lincoln's action by editorializing, "The President has purposely made the proclamation inoperative in all places where we have gained a military footing which makes the slaves accessible. He has proclaimed emancipation only where he has notoriously no power to execute it." The *London Spectator* (October 11, 1862) agreed completely, writing that "the principle is not that a human being cannot justly own another, but that he cannot own him unless he is loyal to the United States" government.

A case can be made that the Emancipation Proclamation was primarily a public relations strategy employed out of desperation because of the utter failure of the federal armies to subdue the rebels during the first eighteen months of the war. Most likely it was designed to encourage the European powers—especially England—to cease trading with the South. . . .

White Northerners' Attitudes Toward Blacks

Northerners discriminated against blacks in cruel and inhumane ways during the 1850s and 1860s. As Alexis de Tocqueville remarked in *Democracy in America*, "The prejudice of race appears to be stronger in the states that have abolished slavery than in those where it still exists."

The *Revised Code of Indiana*, for example, stated in 1862 that "Negroes and mulattos are not allowed to come into the state"; "all contracts with such Negroes and mulattos are declared to be void"; "any person encouraging them to come, or giving them employment, is to be fined from $10 to $500"; "Negroes and mulattos are not to be allowed to vote"; "No Negro, or mulatto having even one-eighth part of Negro blood, shall marry a white person" [with punishment of up to ten years in prison]; and "Negroes and mulattos are not allowed to testify against white persons." This last

Was the Civil War Sir Walter Scott's Fault?

The Civil War has been blamed on many causes, ranging from Northern tariffs to Southern slavery. In the following excerpt from his 1883 book Life on the Mississippi, *author Mark Twain targeted an unusual culprit: the romantic Scottish novelist Sir Walter Scott.*

[Sir Walter Scott] did measureless harm; more real and lasting harm, perhaps, than any other individual that ever wrote. Most of the world has now outlived good part of these harms, though by no means all of them; but in our South they flourish pretty forcefully still. Not so forcefully as half a generation ago, perhaps, but still forcefully. There, the genuine and wholesome civilization of the nineteenth century is curiously confused and commingled with the Walter Scott Middle-Age sham civilization and so you have practical, common-sense, progressive ideas, and progressive works, mixed up with the duel, regulation was an open invitation to the criminal abuse of blacks.

Illinois and Oregon added similar provisions to their state constitutions in 1848 and 1857, respectively. The referendum to amend the Illinois constitution to prohibit the immigration of blacks passed by a margin of more than two to one; the margin was eight to one in Oregon.

Most Northern states that did permit immigration by blacks required them to post a bond of up to $1,000 that would be confiscated by the state if they acted "improperly." To the extent that this provision was enforced, it served as a deterrent to black immigration.

Although New York state helped to elect Lincoln, it overwhelmingly rejected a proposal to allow Negro suffrage. As late as 1869, New York voters defeated equal-suffrage referenda. Between 1849 and 1857, Michigan, Iowa, and Wisconsin overwhelmingly rejected equal-suffrage referenda.

---

the inflated speech, and the jejune romanticism of an absurd past that is dead, and out of charity ought to be buried. But for the Sir Walter disease, the character of the Southerner—or Southron, according to Sir Walter's starchier way of phrasing it—would be wholly modern, in place of modern and mediaeval mixed, and the South would be fully a generation further advanced than it is. It was Sir Walter that made every gentleman in the South a Major or a Colonel, or a General or a Judge, before the war; and it was he, also, that made these gentlemen value these bogus decorations. For it was he that created rank and caste down there, and also reverence for rank and caste, and pride and pleasure in them. Enough is laid on slavery, without fathering upon it these creations and contributions of Sir Walter.

Sir Walter had so large a hand in making Southern character, as it existed before the war, that he is in great measure responsible for the war.

Mark Twain, *Life on the Mississippi*, 1883.

Four Northern states—Illinois, Ohio, Indiana, and Iowa—prohibited Negro testimony in cases where a white person was a party, and Oregon forbade Negroes to own real estate, enter into contracts, or maintain lawsuits.

Restaurants, hotels, libraries, and theaters excluded blacks in the North; black children were excluded from public schools or placed in inferior ones, even though their parents were taxpayers; and most Northern states had established their own state colonization societies for blacks. The public schools in Washington, D.C., were not desegregated until the 1950s—nearly a century after the end of the war.

Racism in the West

Lyman Trumball, a U.S. Senator from Illinois and a close friend of Lincoln's, announced that "there is a very great aversion in the West—I know it to be so in my State—against having free Negroes come among us. Our people want nothing to do with the Negro."

In 1861 Illinois was considered to be part of "the west." Similar anti-black attitudes were apparently pervasive in the "far west"—Iowa, California, Oregon, and Kansas—as well. In *The Frontier against Slavery*, Eugene H. Berwanger documents how "state legislatures, overwhelmed by the fear of being inundated by manumitted slaves or free Negroes from the south, were enacting laws to deprive the Negro immigrants of any semblance of citizenship, to exclude them from the states, and to encourage them to colonize in Africa." "Prejudice against the Negro found special acceptance" in these Northern states.

Racist attitudes toward blacks were pervasive among Northern opinion makers as well as politicians. The *Philadelphia Daily News* editorialized on November 22, 1860, that "it is neither for the good of the colored race nor of our own that they should continue to dwell among us to any considerable extent. The two races can never exist in conjunction except as superior and inferior. . . . The African is naturally the inferior race." The *Niles (Mich.) Republican* wrote on March 30, 1861, that "this government was made for the benefit of the white race . . . and not for *Negroes.*" The *Daily Chicago Times* remarked on December 7, 1860, that "evil, and nothing but evil, has ever followed in the track of this hideous monster, Abolition. . . . Let [the slave] alone—send him back to his master where he belongs."

Making Slavery Tolerable

On January 22, 1861, the *New York Times* announced that it opposed the abolition of slavery. Instead, it proposed that slaves should be allowed to legally marry, to be taught to read, and to invest their money in savings accounts. Those actions should be taken "to ameliorate, rather than to abolish, the Slavery of the Southern States" and would permit slavery to become "a very tolerable system." "We have no more right to meddle with slavery in Georgia, than we have to meddle with monarchy in Europe," declared the *Providence Daily Post* on February 2, 1861. The *Columbus (Ohio) Crisis* added five days later that "we are not Abolitionists nor in favor of Negro equality." The *New York Herald*, the newspaper with the largest circulation in the country at the time, actually sang the praises of slavery on March 7, 1861, when it wrote of how "the immense increase of numbers [of slaves] within so short a time speaks for the good treatment and happy, contented lot of the slaves. They are comfortably fed, housed and clothed, and seldom or never overworked."

The *Philadelphia Inquirer* endorsed Lincoln's colonization ideas on March 11, 1861, when it pointed out that "Hayti lies in the torrid zone, the proper residence of the Negro." "The proposition that the Negro is equal by nature, physically and mentally, to the white man, seems to be so absurd and preposterous, that we cannot conceive how it can be entertained by any intelligent and rational white man," the *Concord (N.H.) Democratic Standard* declared on September 8, 1860. The *Boston Daily Courier* added on September 24, 1860, that "we believe the mulatto to be inferior in capacity, character, and organization to the full-blooded black, and still farther below the standard of the white races."

A Schoolbook Fiction

The foregoing discussion demonstrates that the idea that racially enlightened Northerners marched south and died by the hundreds of thousands for the benefit of black strangers in Alabama and Mississippi, and then marched happily back singing the Battle

Hymn of the Republic—as has been taught in the public schools and portrayed in books, films, and the popular culture in general for more than a century—is simply not credible.

It is conceivable that many white racists in the North nevertheless abhorred the institution of slavery. However, given the attitudes of most Northerners regarding blacks, it is doubtful that their abhorrence of slavery was sufficient motivation for most (not all) of them *to give their lives* on bloody battlefields. It is one thing to proclaim one's opposition to slavery, but quite another to die for it.

I do not deny that slavery was *a* cause of the war, but I maintain that it was one cause among many and that its importance may have been exaggerated.

CHAPTER 2

Were the Actions of the North Legal and Moral?

Chapter Preface

"We are not enemies but friends," Lincoln assured rebellious Southerners in his first inaugural address of March 4, 1861. "We must not be enemies." Astonishingly, Lincoln tried to maintain this conciliatory stance while waging the most deadly and destructive war in American history. Throughout the war, he refused to recognize that secession had even taken place. Since the Union was perpetual, such a break was simply impossible.

In Lincoln's view, the nation was in the throes of an insurrection for which most Southern people were not responsible. As historian Garry Wills put it, "Lincoln . . . thought of Jefferson Davis's army as an outlaw band preying on the South."[1] Lincoln seldom used the word *traitors* to describe Southerners, even those in rebellion. He generally spoke of them as "neighbors" and regarded the South itself as still part of the Union. There was no "war between the states"—at least not in the president's mind. Lincoln sometimes seemed to deny that the Union had any external enemy at all. The war was internal and spiritual, a bitter punishment for the nation's collective failure to live up to its founding ideals:

> And whereas, when our own beloved Country, once, by the blessing of God, united, prosperous and happy, is now afflicted with faction and civil war, it is peculiarly fit for us to recognize the hand of God in this terrible visitation, and in sorrowful remembrance of our own faults and crimes as a nation and as individuals, to humble ourselves before Him, and to pray for His mercy,—to pray that we may be spared further punishment, though most justly deserved.[2]

But for all his soul-searching, Lincoln was a ruthless wartime leader. The legality and morality of his actions and those of his subordinates have often been doubted.

One contentious issue is Lincoln's Emancipation Proclamation of January 1, 1863. Generations of schoolchildren have been taught to revere the Emancipation as somehow sacred, as *the* document that freed the slaves. Generations of historians, on the other hand, have felt compelled to point out that the proclamation did no such thing. It made no claim to free any slaves except in regions under Confederate control—not in slave states loyal to the Union nor in any areas occupied by Union troops.

In faulting Lincoln for not simply emancipating all slaves with a stroke of the pen, critics show an ignorance of legal realities. Slavery was protected by the Constitution, even though that document coyly avoided mentioning the "peculiar institution" by name. Only a constitutional amendment, enacted by Congress and the states, could legally end slavery. As president, Lincoln had no such power. But as a wartime commander in chief, *perhaps* he had the power to proclaim the necessity of freeing slaves in rebellious areas. He could not free slaves anywhere else. Nor could he use the wrongful nature of slavery to justify his proclamation. His only feasible appeal was the military necessity of depriving the South of its labor and adding freedmen to Union forces. Even such a limited emancipation was of questionable legitimacy. Lincoln himself felt unsure of its legality, and historians have debated the issue ever since.

Lincoln's motives in writing the proclamation provoke deeper moral questions. If the document was meant solely for its stated purpose as a necessary wartime measure, it may seem a cold and calculating gesture. If the proclamation was geared mainly to keep Great Britain from intervening on the Confederacy's behalf, it may seem downright cynical. But if it was sincerely intended as the first nail in slavery's coffin, Lincoln's admirers are right in regarding it as profoundly noble.

Such debates about the Emancipation Proclamation lead to other moral and legal questions about Lincoln's wartime actions. In the following remarks, the novelist and historian Gore Vidal echoes many of Lincoln's critics:

> Lincoln found that the bronze thread so idly woven into the Constitution provided him, as commander-in-chief, with the powers of a dictator. So he became dictator. He levied troops without consulting Congress, shut down newspapers, suspended habeas corpus, defied the Supreme Court—all in the name of "military necessity."[3]

According to this view, the man revered for his eloquent pronouncements about democracy and human equality was actually a ruthless tyrant, more devoted to building an American empire than to noble ideals. Critics also question the quality and humanity of Lincoln's military leadership. Rightly or wrongly, the Civil War has been described as the first "total war"—that is, a war in which combatants make any sacrifice and break any rules to achieve a victory. If Lincoln considered his Southern neighbors to be mere victims of Jefferson Davis's outlaw government and army, Union forces nevertheless wreaked terrible havoc upon the South. For example, historians remain divided over whether General Sherman's actions during his march across Georgia were truly necessary or justified.

The issues raised in this chapter will likely be debated for as long as the Civil War is discussed and studied—and indeed, for as long as America finds it necessary to engage in war.

Notes

1. Garry Wills, *Lincoln at Gettysburg: The Words That Remade America.* New York: Simon & Schuster, 1992, p. 133.
2. Abraham Lincoln, Proclamation of a National Fast Day, August 12, 1861.
3. Gore Vidal, *The American Presidency.* Chicago: Odonian, 1999, p. 24.

Viewpoint 1

"Why does the Government reject the Negro? Is he not a man?"

The Union Should Enlist Black Soldiers

Frederick Douglass

Frederick Douglass was born into slavery in Maryland, the son of a slave mother and an unknown white father. Despite the illegality of educating slaves, he managed to learn to read and write while serving as a house slave in Baltimore. He escaped to freedom in 1838 at the age of twenty and settled in Massachusetts. Avoiding recapture, he worked as a laborer until, at an 1841 antislavery convention, he gave an eloquent speech describing his life as a slave. He quickly became the most celebrated African American abolitionist of his time. His autobiographical writings include *The Life and Times of Frederick Douglass*, now recognized as a classic of American literature.

From the very beginning of the Civil War, Douglass sought to persuade Northerners that the war was truly a crusade against slavery, and he yearned for the day when black men could fight for their freedom. In the following 1861 article from his periodical *Douglass' Monthly*, Douglass chastises the North for its reluctance to enlist black soldiers. When black troops were finally recruited into the Union army in 1863, two of Douglass's sons were among the first to enlist.

Frederick Douglass, *Douglass' Monthly*, September 1861.

What upon earth is the matter with the American Government and people? Do they really covet the world's ridicule as well as their own social and political ruin? What are they thinking about, or don't they condescend to think at all? So, indeed, it would seem from their blindness in dealing with the tremendous issue now upon them. Was there ever any thing like it before? They are sorely pressed on every hand by a vast army of slave-holding rebels, flushed with success, and infuriated by the darkest inspirations of a deadly hate, bound to rule or ruin. Washington, the seat of Government, after ten thousand assurances to the contrary, is now positively in danger of falling before the rebel army. Maryland, a little while ago considered safe for the Union, is now admitted to be studded with the materials for insurrection, and which may flame forth at any moment.—Every resource of the nation, whether of men or money, whether of wisdom or strength, could be well employed to avert the impending ruin. Yet most evidently the demands of the hour are not comprehended by the Cabinet or the crowd.

"Send Us Men"

Our Presidents, Governors, Generals and Secretaries are calling, with almost frantic vehemence, for men.—"Men! men! send us men!" they scream, or the cause of the Union is gone, the life of a great nation is ruthlessly sacrificed, and the hopes of a great nation go out in darkness; and yet these very officers, representing the people and Government, steadily and persistently refuse to receive the very class of men which have a deeper interest in the defeat and humiliation of the rebels, than all others.—Men are wanted in Missouri—wanted in Western Virginia, to hold and defend what has been already gained; they are wanted in Texas, and all along the sea coast, and though the Government has at its command a class in the country deeply interested in suppressing the insurrection, it sternly refuses to summon from among the vast multitude a single man, and degrades and insults the whole class by refusing to allow any of their number to defend with their strong arms and brave hearts the national cause. What a spectacle of blind, unreasoning prejudice and pusillanimity is this! The national edifice is on fire. Every man who can carry a bucket of water, or remove a brick, is wanted; but those who have the care of the building, having a profound respect for the feeling of the national burglars who set the building on fire, are determined that the flames shall only be extinguished by Indo-Caucasian hands, and to have the building burnt rather than save it by means of any other. Such is the pride, the stupid prejudice and folly that rules the hour.

Negro Soldiers

Why does the Government reject the Negro? Is he not a man? Can he not wield a sword, fire a gun, march and countermarch, and obey orders like any other? Is there the least reason to believe that a regiment of well-drilled Negroes would deport themselves less soldier-like on the battle field than the raw troops gathered up generally from the towns and cities of the State of New York? We do believe that such soldiers, if allowed now to take up arms in defence of the Government, and made to feel that they are hereafter to be recognized as persons having rights, would set the highest example of order and general good behavior to their fellow soldiers, and in every way add to the national power.

The Union government responded to social and political pressure by recruiting black troops into its army.

If persons so humble as we can be allowed to speak to the President of the United States, we should ask him if this dark and terrible hour of the nation's extremity is a time for consulting a mere vulgar and unnatural prejudice? We should ask him if national preservation and necessity were not better guides in this emergency than either the tastes of the rebels, or the pride and prejudices of the vulgar? We would tell him that General [Andrew] Jackson in a slave State fought side by side with Negroes at New Orleans [against the British in the War of 1812], and like a true man, despising meanness, he bore testimony to their bravery at the close of the war. We would tell him that colored men in Rhode Island and Connecticut performed their full share in the war of the [American] Revolution, and that men of the same color, such as the noble Shields Green, Nathaniel Turner and Denmark Vesey stand ready to peril every thing at the command of the Government. We would tell him that this is no time to fight with one hand, when both are needed; that this is no time to fight only with your white hand, and allow your black hand to remain tied.

Black Confederate Soldiers

Whatever may be the folly and absurdity of the North, the South at least is true and wise. The Southern papers no longer indulge in the vulgar expression, "free n—rs." That class of bipeds are now called "colored residents." The Charleston papers say:

> The colored residents of this city can challenge comparison with their class, in any city or town, in loyalty or devotion to the cause of the South. Many of them individually, and without ostentation, have been contributing liberally, and on Wednesday evening, the 7th inst., a very large meeting was held by them, and a Committee appointed to provide for more efficient aid. The proceedings of the meeting will appear in results hereinafter to be reported.

It is now pretty well established, that there are at the present moment many colored men in the Confederate army doing duty not only as cooks, servants and laborers, but as real soldiers, having muskets on their shoulders, and bullets in their pockets, ready to shoot down loyal troops, and do all that soldiers may to destroy the Federal Government and build up that of the traitors and rebels. There were such soldiers at [the First Battle of] Manassas [on July 21, 1861] and they are probably there still. There is a Negro in the army as well as in the fence, and our Government is likely to find it out before the war comes to an end. That the Negroes are numerous in the rebel army, and do for that army its heaviest work, is beyond question. They have been the chief laborers upon those temporary defences in which the rebels have been able to mow down our men. Negroes helped to build the batteries at Charleston. They relieve their gentlemanly and military masters from the stiffening drudgery of the camp, and devote them to the nimble and dexterous use of arms. Rising above vulgar prejudice, the slaveholding rebel accepts the aid of the black man as readily as that of any other. If a bad cause can do this, why should a good cause be less wisely conducted? We insist upon it, that one black regiment in such a war as this is, without being any more brave and orderly, would be worth to the Government more than two of any other; and that, while the Government continues to refuse the aid of colored men, thus alienating them from the national cause, and giving the rebels the advantage of them, it will not deserve better fortunes than it has thus far experienced.—Men in earnest don't fight with one hand, when they might fight with two, and a man drowning would not refuse to be saved even by a colored hand.

Viewpoint 2

"If this Union cannot be preserved by the white man, . . . there are no conditions upon which it can be saved."

The Union Should Not Enlist Black Soldiers

Garrett Davis

After the outbreak of war, not all the states remaining loyal to the Union were free states: Missouri, Kentucky, Delaware, and Maryland still held slaves. The presence of slave states in the Union was one reason it took so long for emancipation to become the war's principle aim. Representatives of these states vigorously opposed any measure that might threaten the institution of slavery or their authority over their slaves.

By the middle of 1861, the Union army suffered from a severe manpower shortage. On July 9, the Senate began debating a resolution authorizing the president to accept African Americans into military service "for the purpose of constructing entrenchments, or performing camp service, or any other labor, or any war service for which they may be found competent." The last phrase of this resolution—suggesting that black men might serve as soldiers—greatly alarmed Senator Garrett Davis of Ken-

Garrett Davis, address to the U.S. Senate, Washington, DC, July 9, 1861.

tucky, a pro-Union, proslavery Democrat. Putting arms into the hands of blacks, whether freedmen or slaves, was repugnant to him and many of his constituents. The following viewpoint is excerpted from Davis's speech opposing this provision.

I have myself never considered secession a remedy for any evil. I do not now consider it a remedy for any evil, but to have brought upon the country all existing evils; and that, if an accomplished fact, it would prove the fruitful mother of many other evils, of which we have yet had no experience. For my own State, for the South, for the North, for the East, and the West, I have no hope, if secession is triumphant and permanent dissolution takes place. I am for a reconstruction of the Union. I believe the only principle and means by which that reconstruction is possible, is by the employment of the full, legitimate military power of the country, and not by arming slaves and attempting to form a military force of them. . . .

Blacks Can Be Workers, Not Soldiers

From the debate that has sprung up in this Chamber on this subject, it appears to me that there are only two principal matters in the measure proposed about which there is much difference of opinion. The one is the employment of the negro in all camp and military labor, and the other is placing arms in his hands, and forming him into a portion of the soldiery of the United States in the war. To the first proposition I have no objection, and never had any, but to the second I am utterly opposed, and will ever be opposed. . . .

I never heard any Union man in my State or out of it object to the use and the appropriation of negroes by the United States Government, just as other property is applied to their military purposes. The whole of their remonstrance and protest has been against making a discrimination between that and other property by the laws of Congress or by the policy of the war, as the President or his generals might carry it on. When a general is commanding in the field, and he has occasion for the labor of horses and oxen, what does he do? He impresses them into the service of the Army of the United States, and nobody objects. Just so, if that general may need the services of negroes for the purpose of fortifying, or ditching, or rendering any other labor in his camp, or any service whatever, especially that kind which would shield and protect and save the life of the white soldier, I think that general in command would be perfectly authorized so to employ the negro, and I have never heard any man object to such employment; certainly I never made any such objection as that myself. And all this would be done by order of the President, or by our generals commanding, without any act of Congress to authorize it. But when the general has done with the negro, and the negro is no longer useful in his camp for the purpose of labor, or for any other useful purpose, let him be discharged, sent away like other property. I protest against placing arms in his hands and making a soldier of him; and to that line of policy I never will give my consent; nor will my people, although it may be regarded as a matter of very little importance in this Senate what they or I think in relation to this or any other measure of policy of the dominant party. If the State of Kentucky was polled upon the proposition of placing arms in the hands of negroes, I have no doubt to-day that nine hundred and ninety-nine out of every thousand, yea, I believe that the thousandth man would vote against it, and enter up his most solemn remonstrance against it.

An Insult to White Soldiers

Has it come to this, Mr. President, that we cannot command white soldiers enough to fight our battles to put down this rebellion? Whenever we authorize by law of Congress the enrollment of negro soldiers for that purpose, we admit that the white man is whipped in the contest, and that he cannot come out conqueror without making an auxiliary of the negro. I protest against any such degrading position as that. Our countrymen are not reduced to it; and sooner than the white men, the citizens and sovereigns of the United States, would submit to so humiliating an admission as that, one million of additional soldiers would be ready to rush to the battle-field. I believe that if this measure was passed it would weaken our Army; it would weaken the cause of the Union and of the legitimate Government in this contest tenfold as much as it would strengthen it.

Sir, I know the soldiery of the Northwest. They want no negro auxiliaries in this war; they would feel themselves degraded fighting by their side. They feel that the white race are amply strong in numbers, in courage, in all the elements of a martial people, to bring this contest to a close without the ignominy of enlisting the negro as a fellow-soldier. I deny that in the revolutionary war there ever was any considerable organization of negroes. I deny that in the war of 1812 there was ever any organization of negro slaves. I admit that through both those wars, and in the Mexican war, and also in the present war, there have been negro slaves that were waiters upon masters in the armies in whose hands in battle arms have been placed, and who used those arms; but they were in only a very few and exceptional cases an organized soldiery. . . .

I know the negro well; I know his nature. He is, until excited, mild and gentle; he is affectionate and faithful, too; but when his passions have been inflamed and thoroughly aroused, you find him a fiend, a latent tiger fierceness in his heart, and when he becomes excited by a taste of blood he is a demon. Such is the nature of the race; and there never was a servile insurrection in the world where it did not manifest that nature. In the Southampton insurrection a few years ago in Virginia [the 1831 Nat Turner rebellion] the negroes displayed the nature which I have imputed to them. I admit that they do not spring to acts of cruelty and ferocity at once. They have to be schooled awhile to prepare them; they come to such acts step by step, as they did in the island of St. Domingo [Haiti, the site of a violent slave revolt against the French colonial government in the 1790s]. . . .

Constitution Guarantees Slavery

Sir, there is not a man in this body nor in the land that is more deeply devoted to the restoration of the Union than I am, or one who is more attached to the Union and to the Constitution which forms the government of the United States. But when you offer to me and my people a policy and ask us, will you take our measures; will you take general confiscation of the property of all the disloyal; abolition of slavery, the slaves to remain in their localities;

will you agree to our arming them, and making them soldiers to fight the battle of the Constitution, which Constitution guarantied them as property to their owners; will you take all these atrocities? We answer, never! never! never! All we ask, is that the just power of the Government of the United States shall be brought into full requisition to suppress this rebellion. The Union men of the slave States are as ready to cooperate in that just and constitutional war as are the Union men of the free States; but they require that the Constitution—the bond of our Union, the ark of our liberties, without which there can be no freedom in this land—shall be held intact and religiously preserved throughout all the storms of the conflict. They ask no exemption of their property from the same law, the same policy, and the same military measures that you would deal out to any other property. I have a few slaves, and my county possesses upwards of seven thousand. If it were necessary to-morrow, to prevent the consummation of this revolution and the disruption of the Union, that those seven thousand slaves should be manumitted, there is not one of them belonging to a Union man who would not be surrendered just as cheerfully as sacrifice for so great an end ever was made by a loyal heart to the cause of his country. But we believe and know that there is no such necessity; there is no such sacrifice required at our hands. On the other hand, we believe and know that the policy so madly urged in the two Houses of Congress by some of the extreme men is fatal, or eminently mischievous to the purposes they profess to have in view. Instead of weakening and subduing the rebels, it would strengthen them. . . .

No Necessity for Black Soldiers

If this Union cannot be preserved by the white man, making him the soldier and the hero of the battle for the Union, there are no conditions upon which it can be saved. But, sir, it can be rescued upon that noble condition; it ought not to be attempted on any other. If you put arms in the hands of the negroes and make them feel their power and impress them with their former slavery, wrongs, and injustice, and arm them, as [General David] Hunter promises, to the number of fifty thousand, you will whet their fiendish passions, make them the destroying scourge of the cotton States, and you will bring upon the country a condition of things what will render restoration hopeless. There is no necessity for it; there can be none. Exhaust the energies, the patriotism, and the resources of the white man; at least tax them further, and yet further, and whenever the time comes and you demonstrate to slave-holding Union men that by the sacrifice of their slaves the Union can be restored and the Constitution can be preserved, and that there shall be but one American empire whose arch shall span the continent from ocean to ocean, and that sacrifice will be unhesitatingly made.

But there is no such stress upon us. It is an inglorious, ignoble, and a cowardly admission that there is any such stress or necessity as that. Why, sir, do you not perceive that the Englishman, the Frenchman, and the Spaniard are already beginning to contemn and spit upon you? Yesterday, or before this rebellion, the name of American might have stood against the world; now it is so poor that none will even do it reverence. That contempt and degradation of our country, that ignoble impress will go on rapidly increasing—yes, sir, it will go on irretrievably to its miserable, degrading consummation, whenever you agree to call in regiments, brigades, divisions, and army corps of negroes into the field. I implore you to use the negro for no such purpose. Wherever you can make him labor, wherever you can make him useful without putting arms in his hands, employ him; there can be no just objection to it. In a particular state of the case, where there was a small corps or a large corps hard pressed, and there were negroes about, and they could be made to swab the cannon, to load the cannon, or fire guns, and to use the cutlass, or any other weapon, in such an emergency, use him; but do not make occasion to use him. Do not organize him as a part of our Army.

Viewpoint 3

"Read the proclamation for it is the most important of any to which the President of the United States has ever signed his name."

The Emancipation Proclamation Ennobles the Union Cause

Frederick Douglass

The escaped slave Frederick Douglass was one of the most influential abolitionist leaders of his time. In his speeches and writings, Douglass probably did as much as President Lincoln to turn the Civil War into a crusade against slavery. Early in the war, Douglass was Lincoln's gadfly, castigating the president for his reluctance to address the issue of emancipation. But Douglass eventually became Lincoln's trusted adviser. Historian David W. Blight, in his book *Race and Reunion*, describes Douglass as "the President's unacknowledged and unpaid alter ego, the intellectual godfather of the Gettysburg Address."

On September 22, 1862, President Lincoln issued his preliminary Emancipation Proclamation. This ultimatum demanded that the Confederate states return to the Union by January or

Frederick Douglass, *Douglass' Monthly*, October 1862.

else all slaves in rebel territories would be declared free. The Confederate states refused to return, and Lincoln issued his final Emancipation Proclamation on New Year's Day of 1863.

The Emancipation Proclamation has drawn criticism ever since it was written. Critics have long pointed out that it did not effectively free any slaves at all—at least not immediately. But in the following October 1862 article from his periodical *Douglass' Monthly*, Douglass argues that the preliminary Emancipation Proclamation has changed the meaning of the war and spelled slavery's doom.

Common sense, the necessities of the war, to say nothing of the dictation of justice and humanity have at last prevailed. We shout for joy that we live to record this righteous decree. *Abraham Lincoln*, President of the United States, Commander-in-Chief of the army and navy, in his own peculiar, cautious, forbearing and hesitating way, slow, but we hope sure, has, while the loyal heart was near breaking with despair, proclaimed and declared: "*That on the First of January, in the Year of Our Lord One Thousand, Eight Hundred and Sixty-three, All Persons Held as Slaves Within Any State or Any Designated Part of a State, The People Whereof Shall Then be in Rebellion Against the United States, Shall be Thenceforward and Forever Free.*" "Free forever" oh! long enslaved millions, whose cries have so vexed the air and sky, suffer on a few more days in sorrow, the hour of your deliverance draws nigh! Oh! Ye millions of free and loyal men who have earnestly sought to free your bleeding country from the dreadful ravages of revolution and anarchy, lift up now your voices with joy and thanksgiving for with freedom to the slave will come peace and safety to your country. President Lincoln has embraced in this proclamation the law of Congress passed more than six months ago, prohibiting the employment of any part of the army and naval forces of the United States, to return fugitive slaves to their masters, commanded all officers of the army and navy to respect and obey its provisions. He has still further declared his intention to urge upon the Legislature of all the slave States not in rebellion the immediate or gradual abolishment of slavery. But read the proclamation for it is the most important of any to which the President of the United States has ever signed his name.

Lincoln's Signature

Opinions will widely differ as to the practical effect of this measure upon the war. All that class at the North who have not lost their affection for slavery will regard the measure as the very worst that could be devised, and as likely to lead to endless mischief. All their plans for the future have been projected with a view to a reconstruction of the American Government upon the basis of compromise between slaveholding and non-slaveholding States. The thought of a country unified in sentiments, objects and ideas, has not entered into their political calculations, and hence this newly declared policy of the Government, which contemplates one glorious homogeneous people, doing away at a blow with the whole class of compromisers and corrupters, will meet their stern opposition. Will that opposition prevail? Will it lead the President to reconsider and retract? Not a word of it. Abraham Lincoln may be slow, Abraham Lincoln may desire peace even at the price of leaving our terrible national sore untouched, to fester on for generations, but Abraham Lincoln is not the man to reconsider, retract and contradict words and purposes solemnly proclaimed over his official signature.

No Stepping Backward

The careful, and we think, the slothful deliberation which he has observed in reaching this obvious policy, is a guarantee against retraction. But even if the temper and spirit of the President himself were other than what they are, events greater than the President, events which have slowly wrung this proclamation from him may be relied on to carry him forward in the same direction. To look back now would only load him with heavier evils, while diminishing his ability, for overcoming those with which he now has to contend. To recall his proclamation would only increase rebel pride, rebel sense of power and would be hailed as a direct admission of weakness on the part of the Federal Government, while it would cause heaviness of heart and depression of national enthusiasm all over the loyal North and West. No, Abraham Lincoln will take no step backward. His word has gone out over the country and the world, giving joy and gladness to the friends of freedom and progress wherever those words are read, and he will stand by them, and carry them out to the letter. If he has taught us to confide in nothing else, he has taught us to confide in his word. The want of Constitutional power, the want of military power, the tendency of the measure to intensify Southern hate, and to exasperate the rebels, the tendency to drive from him all that class of Democrats at the North, whose loyalty has been conditioned on his restoring the union as it was, slavery and all, have all been considered, and he has taken his ground notwithstanding. The President doubtless saw, as we see, that it is not more absurd to talk about restoring the union, without hurting slavery, than restoring the union without hurting the rebels. As to exasperating the South, there can be no more in the cup than the cup will hold, and that was full already. The whole situation having been carefully scanned, before Mr. Lincoln could be made to budge an inch, he will now stand his ground. Border State influence, and the influence of half-loyal men, have been exerted and have done their worst. The end of these two influences is implied in this proclamation. Hereafter, the inspiration as well as the men and the money for carrying on the war will come from the North, and not from half-loyal border States.

Impact at Home and Abroad

The effect of this paper upon the disposition of Europe will be great and increasing. It changes the character of the war in European eyes and gives it an important principle as an object, instead of national pride and interest. It recognizes and declares the real nature of the contest, and places the North on the side of justice and civilization, and the rebels on the side of robbery and barbarism. It will disarm all purpose on the part of European Government to intervene in favor of the rebels and thus cast off at a blow one source of rebel power. All through the war thus far, the rebel ambassadors in foreign countries have been able to silence all expression of sympathy with the North as to slavery. With much more than a show of truth, they said that the Federal Government, no more than the Confederate Government, contemplated the abolition of slavery.

But will not this measure be frowned upon by our officers and men in the field? We have heard of many thousands who have resolved that they will throw up their commissions and lay down their arms, just so soon as they are required to carry on a war against slavery. Making all allowances for exaggeration there are doubtless far too many of this sort in the loyal army. Putting this kind of loyalty and patriotism to the test, will be one of the best collateral effects of the measure. Any man who leaves the field on such a ground will be an argument in favor of the proclamation, and will prove that his heart has been more with slavery than with his country. Let the army be cleansed from all such pro-slavery vermin, and its health and strength will be greatly improved. But there can be no reason to fear the loss of many officers or men by resignation or desertion. We have no doubt that the measure was brought to the attention of most of our leading Generals, and blind as some of them have seemed to be in the earlier part of the war, most of them have seen enough to convince them that there

"Thenceforward, and Forever Free"

The following words appear in both the preliminary and final versions of Lincoln's Emancipation Proclamation. As the U.S. chief executive, Lincoln had no power to interfere with the institution of slavery, but as a wartime commander in chief, he felt he could make a gesture toward emancipation. Constitutional constraints explain why Lincoln liberated slaves only in rebel territories—and also explains his legalistic, calculating tone.

That on the first day of January, in the year of our Lord one thousand eight hundred and sixty-three, all persons held as slaves within any State or designated part of a State, the people whereof shall then be in rebellion against the United States, shall be then, thenceforward, and forever free; and the Executive Government of the United States, including the military and naval authority thereof, will recognize and maintain the can be no end to this war that does not end slavery. At any rate, we may hope that for every pro-slavery man that shall start from the ranks of our loyal army, there will be two anti-slavery men to fill up the vacancy, and in this war one truly devoted to the cause of Emancipation is worth two of the opposite sort.

Two Necessary Conditions

Whether slavery will be abolished in the manner now proposed by President Lincoln, depends of course upon two conditions, the first specified and the second implied. The first is that the slave States shall be in rebellion on and after the first day of January 1863 and the second is we must have the ability to put down that rebellion. About the first there can be very little doubt. The South is thoroughly in earnest and confident. It has staked everything upon the rebellion. Its experience thus far in the field has rather increased its hopes of final success than diminished them. Its armies now hold us at bay at all points, and the war is confined to the border States slave and free. If Richmond were in our hands

---

freedom of such persons, and will do no act or acts to repress such persons, or any of them, in any efforts they may make for their actual freedom.

That the Executive will, on the first day of January aforesaid, by proclamation, designate the States and parts of States, if any, in which the people thereof, respectively, shall then be in re-bellion against the United States; and the fact that any State, or the people thereof, shall on that day be, in good faith, repre-sented in the Congress of the United States by members cho-sen thereto at elections whereto a majority of the qualified vot-ers of such State shall have participated, shall, in the absence of strong countervailing testimony, be deemed conclusive evi-dence that such State, and the people thereof, are not then in rebellion against the United States.

Abraham Lincoln, Emancipation Proclamation, January 1, 1863.

and Virginia at our mercy, the vast regions beyond would still remain to be subdued. But the rebels confront us on the Potomac, the Ohio, and the Mississippi. Kentucky, Maryland, Missouri, and Virginia are in debate on the battlefields and their people are divided by the line which separates treason from loyalty. In short we are yet, after eighteen months of war, confined to the outer margin of the rebellion. We have scarcely more than touched the surface of the terrible evil. It has been raising large quantities of food during the past summer. While the masters have been fighting abroad, the slaves have been busy working at home to supply them with the means of continuing the struggle. They will not [back] down at the bidding of this Proclamation, but may be safely relied upon till January and long after January. A month or two will put an end to general fighting for the winter. When the leaves fall we shall hear again of bad roads, winter quarters and spring campaigns. The South which has thus far withstood our arms will not fall at once before our pens. All fears for the abolition of slavery arising from this apprehension may be dismissed. Whoever, therefore, lives to see the first day of next January, should Abraham Lincoln be then alive and President of the United States, may confidently look in the morning papers for the final proclamation, granting freedom, and freedom forever, to all slaves within the rebel States.

Union Power

On the next point nothing need be said. We have full power to put down the rebellion. Unless one man is more than a match for four, unless the South breeds braver and better men than the North, unless slavery is more precious than liberty, unless a just cause kindles a feebler enthusiasm than a wicked and villainous one, the men of the loyal States will put down this rebellion and slavery, and all the sooner will they put down that rebellion by coupling slavery with that object. Tenderness towards slavery has been the loyal weakness during the war. Fighting the slaveholders with one hand and holding the slaves with the other, has been fairly tried and has failed. We have now inaugurated a wiser and better policy, a policy which is better for the loyal cause than an hundred thousand armed men. The Star Spangled Banner is now the harbinger of Liberty and the millions in bondage, inured to hardships, accustomed to toil, ready to suffer, ready to fight, to dare and to die, will rally under that banner wherever they see it gloriously unfolded to the breeze. Now let the Government go forward in its mission of Liberty as the only condition of peace and union, by weeding out the army and navy of all such officers as the late Col. [Dixon] Miles, whose sympathies are now known to have been with the rebels. Let only the men who assent heartily to the wisdom and the justice of the anti-slavery policy of the Government be lifted into command; let the black man have an arm as well as a heart in this war, and the tide of battle which has thus far only waved backward and forward, will steadily set in our favor. The rebellion suppressed, slavery abolished, and America will, higher than ever, sit as a queen among the nations of the earth.

To Work

Now for the work. During the interval between now and next January, let every friend of the long enslaved bondman do his utmost in swelling the tide of anti-slavery sentiment, by writing, speaking, money and example. Let our aim be to make the North a unit in favor of the President's policy, and see to it that our voices and votes, shall forever extinguish that latent and malignant sentiment at the North, which has from the first cheered on the rebels in their atrocious crimes against the union, and has systematically sought to paralyze the national arm in striking down the slaveholding rebellion. We are ready for this service or any other, in this, we trust the last struggle with the monster slavery.

Viewpoint 4

*"This proclamation is also an authentic statement
by the Government of the United States of its
inability to subjugate the South by force of arms."*

The Emancipation Proclamation Vindicates the Confederacy

Jefferson Davis

If President Lincoln's Emancipation Proclamation of January 1,
1863, was controversial in the North, it was universally despised
in the Confederacy. The Southern states had seceded because of
their apprehensions about Lincoln's antislavery views, and now
those apprehensions were fully realized. The president's claims
that he did not intend to interfere with slavery had proven
disingenuous at last; he had really meant his 1858 declaration
that the Union could not "endure permanently half slave and
half free." The South now had to fight for lasting independence
if it hoped to preserve the institution of slavery.

The Confederacy's first and only president, Jefferson Davis,
had had a distinguished career before the war. A West Point
graduate and Mexican War hero, he had been U.S. secretary of

Jefferson Davis, message to the Confederate Congress, January 12, 1863.

war under President Franklin Pierce and a U.S. representative and senator from Mississippi. Although initially opposed to secession, he soon changed his mind. He resigned from the U.S. Senate twelve days after his home state of Mississippi seceded on January 9, 1861. On February 18, he was inaugurated as president of the Confederate States of America.

The following viewpoint is excerpted from Davis's special message to the Confederate Congress on January 12, 1863. Here Davis denounces Lincoln's Emancipation Proclamation, asserting that it vindicates the Confederacy's wisdom in withdrawing from the Union.

The public journals of the North have been received, containing a proclamation, dated on the 1st day of the present month [January 1863], signed by the President of the United States, in which he orders and declares all slaves within ten of the States of the Confederacy to be free, except such as are found within certain districts now occupied in part by the armed forces of the enemy. We may well leave it to the instincts of that common humanity which a beneficent Creator has implanted in the breasts of our fellowmen of all countries to pass judgment on a measure by which several millions of human beings of an inferior race, peaceful and contented laborers in their sphere, are doomed to extermination, while at the same time they are encouraged to a general assassination of their masters by the insidious recommendation "to abstain from violence unless in necessary self-defense." Our own detestation of those who have attempted the most execrable measure recorded in the history of guilty man is tempered by profound contempt for the impotent rage which it discloses. So far as regards the action of this Government on such criminals as may attempt its execution, I confine myself to informing you that I shall, unless in your wisdom you deem some other course more expedient, deliver to the several State authorities all commissioned officers of the United States that may hereafter be captured by our forces in any of the States embraced in the proclamation, that they may be dealt with in accordance with the laws of those States providing for the punishment of criminals engaged in exciting servile insurrection. The enlisted soldiers I shall continue to treat as unwilling instruments in the commission of these crimes, and shall direct their discharge and return to their homes on the proper and usual parole.

The Designs of Lincoln

In its political aspect this measure possesses great significance, and to it in this light I invite your attention. It affords to our whole people the complete and crowning proof of the true nature of the designs of the party which elevated to power the present occupant of the Presidential chair at Washington and which sought to conceal its purpose by every variety of artful device and by the perfidious use of the most solemn and repeated pledges on every possible occasion. . . .

The people of this Confederacy, then, cannot fail to receive this proclamation as the fullest vindication of their own sagacity in foreseeing the uses to which the dominant party in the United States intended from the beginning to apply their power, nor can they cease to remember with devout thankfulness that it is to their own vigilance in resisting the first stealthy progress of approaching despotism that they owe their escape from consequences now apparent to the most skeptical. This proclamation will have another salutary effect in calming the fears of those who have constantly evinced the apprehension that this war might end by some reconstruction of the old Union or some renewal of close political relations with the United States. These fears have never been shared by me, nor have I ever been able to perceive on what basis they could rest. But the proclamation affords the fullest guarantee of the impossibility of such a result; it has established a state of things which can lead to but one of three possible consequences—the extermination of the slaves, the exile of the whole white population from the Confederacy, or absolute and total separation of these States from the United States.

The North Must Prepare to Submit

This proclamation is also an authentic statement by the Government of the United States of its inability to subjugate the South by force of arms, and as such must be accepted by neutral nations, which can no longer find any justification in withholding our just claims to formal recognition. It is also in effect an intimation to the people of the North that they must prepare to submit to a separation, now become inevitable, for that people are too acute not to understand a restoration of the Union has been rendered forever impossible by the adoption of a measure which from its very nature neither admits of retraction nor can coexist with union.

Viewpoint 5

"And thus, sir, it is that the freedom of the negro is to be purchased . . . at the sacrifice of every right of the white men of the United States."

Lincoln Is Assuming Unconstitutional and Tyrannical Powers

Clement L. Vallandigham

Ohio representative Clement L. Vallandigham was a proslavery Democrat with strong Southern sympathies. He bitterly opposed Lincoln's war policies from the start, especially the president's suspension of habeas corpus, the constitutional protection against imprisonment without just cause.

In 1863, Congress passed an act upholding the suspension of habeas corpus. Congress also passed a conscription bill allowing the administration to draft men between the ages of twenty and forty-five into military service. In fiery speeches before Congress and throughout his home state, Vallandigham attacked both measures and the war itself. In May 1863, he was arrested, tried, and found guilty of expressing treasonable sympathies. Vallandigham was initially sentenced to imprisonment, but Lincoln commuted his sentence to banishment to the Confederacy. When the South gave him scant welcome, Vallandigham made

Clement L. Vallandigham, address to the U.S. House of Representatives, Washington, DC, February 23, 1863.

his way to Canada. He eventually returned illegally to Ohio, where he continued his antiwar, antiadministration efforts. In 1864, he helped write the national Democratic platform, which contained a strong denunciation of the war.

The following viewpoint is excerpted from a speech Vallandigham delivered to the House of Representatives on February 23, 1863—three months before his arrest. Here he bitterly denounces Congress's conscription bill and the habeas corpus act. The "Sir" whom Vallandigham repeatedly addresses is the Speaker of the House.

Talk to me, indeed, of the leniency of the Executive! too few arrests! too much forbearance by those in power! Sir, it is the people who have been too lenient. They have submitted to your oppressions and wrongs as no free people ought ever to submit. But the day of patient endurance has gone by at last. Mistake them not. They will be lenient no longer. Abide by the Constitution, stand by the laws, restore the Union, if *you* can restore it—not by force—you have tried that and failed. Try some other method now—the ancient, the approved, the reasonable way—the way in which the Union was first made. . . .

For what was the Union ordained? As a splendid edifice, to attract the gaze and admiration of the world? As a magnificent temple—a stupendous superstructure of marble and iron, like this Capitol, upon whose lofty dome the bronzed image—hollow and inanimate—of Freedom is soon to stand erect in colossal mockery, while the true spirit, the living Goddess of Liberty, veils her eyes and turns away her face in sorrow, because, upon the altar established here, and dedicated by our fathers to her worship—you, a false and most disloyal priesthood, offer up, night and morning, the mingled sacrifices of servitude and despotism? No, sir. It was for the sake of the altar, the service, the religion, the devotees, that the temple of the Union was first erected; and when these are all gone, let the edifice itself perish. Never—never—never will the people consent to lose their own personal and political rights and liberties, to the end that you may delude and mock them with the splendid unity of despotism.

Abuses of Power

Sir, what are the bills which have passed, or are still before the House? The bill to give the President the entire control of the currency—the purse—of the country. A tax-bill to clothe him with power over the whole property of the country. A bill to put all power in his hands over the personal liberties of the people. A bill to indemnify him, and all under him, for every act of oppression and outrage already consummated. A bill to enable him to suspend the writ of *habeas corpus*, in order to justify or protect him, and every minion of his, in the arrests which he or they may choose to make—arrests, too, for mere opinion's sake. Sir, some two hundred years ago, men were burned at the stake, subjected to the horrors of the Inquisition, to all the tortures that the devilish ingenuity of man could invent—for what? For opinions on questions of religion—of man's duty and relation to his God. And now, today, for opinions on questions political, under a free government, in a country whose liberties were purchased by our fathers by seven years' outpouring of blood, and expenditure of treasure—we have lived to see men, the born heirs of this precious inheritance, subjected to arrest and cruel imprisonment at the caprice of a President, or a secretary, or a constable. And, as if that were not enough, a bill is introduced here, today, and pressed forward to a vote, with the right of debate, indeed—-extorted from you by the minority—but without the right to amend, with no more than the mere privilege of protest—a bill which enables the President to bring under his power, as Commander-in-chief, every man in the United States between the ages of twenty and forty-five—three millions of men. And, as if not satisfied with that, this bill provides, further, that every other citizen, man, woman, and child, under twenty years of age and over forty-five, including those that may be exempt between these ages, shall be also, at the mercy—so far as his personal liberty is concerned—of some miserable "provost-marshal" with the rank of a captain of cavalry, who is never to see service in the field. . . .

The Price of Black Freedom

What is it, sir, but a bill to abrogate the Constitution, to repeal all existing laws, to destroy all rights, to strike down the judiciary, and erect, upon the ruins of civil and political liberty, a stupendous superstructure of despotism. And for what? To enforce law? No, sir. It is admitted now, by the legislation of Congress, and by the two proclamations of the President; it is admitted by common consent, that the war is for the abolition of negro slavery, to secure freedom to the black man. You tell me, some of you, I know, that it is so prosecuted because this is the only way to restore the Union; but others openly and candidly confess that the purpose of the prosecution of the war is to abolish slavery. And thus, sir, it is that the freedom of the negro is to be purchased, under this bill, at the sacrifice of every right of the white men of the United States. . . .

Tyranny Against the Constitution

What have we lived to hear in America daily, not in political harangues, or the press only, but in official proclamations and in bills in Congress! Yes, your high officials talk now of "treasonable practices," as glibly "as girls of thirteen do of puppy dogs." Treasonable practices! Disloyalty! Who imported these precious phrases, and gave them a legal settlement here? Your Secretary of War [Edwin M. Stanton]. He it was who, by command of our most noble President, authorized every marshal, every sheriff, every township constable, or city policeman, in every State in the Union, to fix, in his own imagination, what he might choose to call a treasonable or disloyal practice, and then to arrest any citizen at his discretion, without an accusing oath, and without due process, or any process of law. And now, sir, all this monstrous tyranny, against the whole spirit and the very letter of the Constitution, is to be deliberately embodied in an Act of Congress! Your petty provost-marshals are to determine what treasonable practices are, and "inquire into," detect, spy out, eavesdrop, ensnare, and then inform, report to the chief spy at Washington. These, sir, are now to be our American liberties under your Administration. There is not a crowned head in Europe who would venture on such an experiment.

Viewpoint 6

"Must I shoot a simple-minded soldier boy who deserts, while I must not touch a hair of a wiley agitator who induces him to desert?"

Extraordinary Measures in Wartime Are Justified

Abraham Lincoln

According to the U.S. Constitution, "the Privilege of the Writ of Habeas Corpus shall not be suspended, unless when in Cases of Rebellion or Invasion the Public Safety may require it." In 1861, President Abraham Lincoln relied on this passage to suspend habeas corpus—the protection against imprisonment without trial and due process. Lincoln's decision led to the arrests of thousands of war opponents.

Did Lincoln have the right to suspend habeas corpus? This question remains controversial even today. Many of Lincoln's contemporaries—especially Democrats—were outraged. Although the war was clearly a case of "Rebellion or Invasion," Lincoln's opponents insisted that only Congress, not the president, had the prerogative to suspend habeas corpus.

The arrest of Ohio representative Clement L. Vallandigham in May 1863 for expressing views that were deemed treasonous set

Abraham Lincoln, letter to Erastus Corning and others, June 12, 1863.

off a storm of protest. That same month, a group of Democrats meeting in Albany, New York, wrote a petition protesting Vallandigham's arrest and Lincoln's suspension of habeas corpus. They set forth their arguments as a series of resolutions. Lincoln replied to this petition in a famous letter of June 12, 1863, excerpted in the following viewpoint.

Gentlemen Your letter of May 19th. inclosing the resolutions of a public meeting held at Albany, N.Y., on the 16th. of the same month, was received several days ago.

The resolutions, as I understand them, are resolvable into two propositions—first, the expression of a purpose to sustain the cause of the Union, to secure peace through victory, and to support the administration in every constitutional, and lawful measure to suppress the rebellion; and secondly, a declaration of censure upon the administration for supposed unconstitutional action such as the making of military arrests.

And, from the two propositions a third is deduced, which is, that the gentlemen composing the meeting are resolved on doing their part to maintain our common government and country, despite the folly or wickedness, as they may conceive, of any administration. This position is eminently patriotic, and as such, I thank the meeting, and congratulate the nation for it. My own purpose is the same; so that the meeting and myself have a common object, and can have no difference, except in the choice of means or measures, for effecting that object.

And here I ought to close this paper, and would close it, if there were no apprehension that more injurious consequences, than any merely personal to myself, might follow the censures systematically cast upon me for doing what, in my view of duty, I could not forbear. The resolutions promise to support me in every constitutional and lawful measure to suppress the rebellion; and I have not knowingly employed, nor shall knowingly employ, any other. But the meeting, by their resolutions, assert and argue, that certain military arrests and proceedings following them for which I am ultimately responsible, are unconstitutional. I think they are not. The resolutions quote from the constitution, the definition of treason; and also the limiting safe-guards and guarrantees therein provided for the citizen, on trials for treason, and on his being held to answer for capital or otherwise infamous crimes, and, in criminal prossecutions, his right to a speedy and public trial by an impartial jury. They proceed to resolve "That these safe-guards of the rights of the citizen against the pretentions of arbitrary power, were intended more *especially* for his protection in times of civil commotion." And, apparently, to demonstrate the proposition, the resolutions proceed "They were secured substantially to the English people, *after* years of protracted civil war, and were adopted into our constitution at the *close* of the revolution." Would not the demonstration have been better, if it could have been truly said that these safe-guards had been adopted, and applied *during* the civil wars and *during* our revolution, instead of *after* the one, and at the *close* of the other. I too am devotedly for them *after* civil war, and *before* civil war, and at all times "except when, in cases of Rebellion or Invasion, the public Safety may require" their suspension. . . .

But these provisions of the constitution have no application to the case we have in hand, because the arrests complained of were not made for treason—that is, not for *the* treason defined in the constitution, and upon the conviction of which, the punishment is death—nor yet were they made to hold persons to answer for any capital, or otherwise infamous crimes; nor were the proceedings following, in any constitutional or legal sense, "criminal prossecutions." The arrests were made on totally different grounds, and the proceedings following, accorded with the grounds of the arrests. Let us consider the real case with which we are dealing, and apply to it the parts of the constitution plainly made for such cases.

Roots of Rebellion

Prior to my instalation here it had been inculcated that any State had a lawful right to secede from the national Union; and that it would be expedient to exercise the right, whenever the devotees of the doctrine should fail to elect a President to their own liking. I was elected contrary to their liking; and accordingly, so far as it was legally possible, they had taken seven states out of the Union, had seized many of the United States Forts, and had fired upon the United States' Flag, all before I was inaugerated; and, of course, before I had done any official act whatever. The rebellion, thus began soon ran into the present civil war, and, in certain respects, it began on very unequal terms between the parties. The insurgents had been preparing for it more than thirty years, while the government had taken no steps to resist them. The former had carefully considered all the means which could be turned to their account. It undoubtedly was a well pondered reliance with them that in their own unrestricted effort to destroy Union, constitution, and law, all together, the government would, in great degree, be restrained by the same constitution and law, from arresting their progress. Their sympathizers pervaded all departments of the government, and nearly all communities of the people. From this material, under cover of "Liberty of speech" "Liberty of the press" and "Habeas corpus" they hoped to keep on foot amongst us a most efficient corps of spies, informers, suppliers, and aiders and abettors of their cause in a thousand ways. They knew that in times such as they were inaugerating, by the constitution itself, the Habeas corpus might be suspended; but they also knew they had friends who would make a question as to *who* was to suspend it; meanwhile their spies and others might remain at large to help on their cause. Or if, as has happened, the executive should suspend the writ, without ruinous waste of time, instances of arresting innocent persons might occur, as are always liken to occur in such cases; and then a clamor could be raised in regard to this, which might be, at least, of some service to the insurgent cause. It needed no very keen perception to discover this part of the enemies' programme, so soon as by open hostilities their machinery was fairly put in motion. Yet, thoroughly imbued with a reverence for the guarranteed rights of individuals, I was slow to adopt the strong measures, which by degrees I have been forced to regard as being within the exceptions of the constitution, and as indispensable to the public Safety. Nothing is better known to history than that courts of justice are utterly incompetent to such cases. Civil courts are organized chiefly for trials of individuals, or, at most, a few individuals acting in concert; and this in quiet times, and on charges of crimes well defined in the law. Even in times of peace, bands of horse-thieves and robbers frequently grow too numerous and powerful for the ordinary courts of justice. But what comparison, in numbers, have such bands ever borne to the insurgent sympa- thizers even in many of the loyal states? Again, a jury too fre- quently have at least one member, more ready to hang the panel than to hang the traitor. And yet again, he who dissuades one man from volunteering, or induces one soldier to desert, weakens the Union cause as much as he who kills a union soldier in battle. Yet this dissuasion, or inducement, may be so conducted as to be no defined crime of which any civil court would take cognizance.

Too Few Arrests, Not Too Many

Ours is a case of Rebellion—so called by the resolutions before me—in fact, a clear, flagrant, and gigantic case of Rebellion; and the provision of the constitution that "The previlege of the writ of Habeas Corpus shall not be suspended, unless when in cases of Rebellion or Invasion, the public Safety may require it" is *the* pro- vision which specially applies to our present case. This provision plainly attests the understanding of those who made the consti- tution that ordinary courts of justice are inadequate to "cases of Rebellion"—attests their purpose that in such cases, men may be held in custody whom the courts acting on ordinary rules, would discharge. Habeas Corpus, does not discharge men who are proved to be guilty of defined crime; and its suspension is allowed by the constitution on purpose that, men may be arrested and held, who can not be proved to be guilty of defined crime "when, in cases of Rebellion or Invasion the public Safety may require it." This is precisely our present case—a case of Rebellion, wherein the public Safety does require the suspension. Indeed, arrests by process of courts, and arrests in cases of rebellion, do not proceed altogether upon the same basis. The former is directed at the small per centage of ordinary and continuous perpetration of crime; while the latter is directed at sudden and extensive uprisings against the government, which, at most, will succeed or fail, in no great length of time. In the latter case, arrests are made, not so much for what has been done, as for what probably would be done. The latter is more for the preventive, and less for the vindictive, than the former. In such cases the purposes of men are much more easily understood, than in cases of ordinary crime. The man who stands by and says nothing, when the peril of his government is discussed, can not be misunderstood. If not hindered, he is sure to help the enemy. Much more, if he talks ambiguously—talks for his country with "buts" and "ifs" and "ands." . . . I think the time not unlikely to come when I shall be blamed for having made too few arrests rather than too many. . . .

Vallandigham's Offense

Take the particular case mentioned by the meeting. It is asserted in substance that Mr. Vallandigham was by a military commander, seized and tried "for no other reason than words addressed to a public meeting, in criticism of the course of the administration, and in condemnation of the military orders of that general." Now, if there be no mistake about this—if this assertion is the truth and the whole truth—if there was no other reason for the arrest, then I concede that the arrest was wrong. But the arrest, as I understand, was made for a very different reason. Mr. Vallandigham avows his hostility to the war on the part of the Union; and his arrest was made because he was laboring, with some effect, to prevent the raising of troops, to encourage desertions from the army, and to leave the rebellion without an adequate military force to suppress it. He was not arrested because he was damaging the political prospects of the administration, or the personal interests of the commanding general; but because he was damaging the army, upon the existence, and vigor of which, the life of the nation depends. He was warring upon the military; and this gave the military constitutional jurisdiction to lay hands upon him. If Mr. Vallandigham was not damaging the military power of the country, then his arrest was made on mistake of fact, which I would be glad to correct, on reasonably satisfactory evidence.

Deserters, Agitators, and Public Safety

I understand the meeting, whose resolutions I am considering, to be in favor of suppressing the rebellion by military force—by armies. Long experience has shown that armies can not be maintained unless desertion shall be punished by the severe penalty of death. The case requires, and the law and the constitution, sanction this punishment. Must I shoot a simple-minded soldier boy who deserts, while I must not touch a hair of a wiley agitator who induces him to desert? This is none the less injurious when effected by getting a father, or brother, or friend, into a public meeting, and there working upon his feeling, till he is persuaded to write the soldier boy, that he is fighting in a bad cause, for a wicked administration of a contemptable government, too weak to arrest and punish him if he shall desert. I think that in such a case, to silence the agitator, and save the boy, is not only constitutional, but, withal, a great mercy.

If I be wrong on this question of constitutional power, my error lies in believing that certain proceedings are constitutional when, in cases of rebellion or Invasion, the public Safety requires them, which would not be constitutional when, in absence of rebellion or invasion, the public Safety does not require them—in other words that the constitution is not in its application in all respects the same, in cases of Rebellion or invasion, involving the public Safety, as it is in times of profound peace and public security. The constitution itself makes the distinction; and I can no more be persuaded that the government can constitutionally take no strong measure in time of rebellion, because it can be shown that the same could not be lawfully taken in time of peace, than I can be persuaded that a particular drug is not good medicine for a sick man, because it can be shown to not be good food for a well one. Nor am I able to appreciate the danger, apprehended by the meeting, that the American people will, by means of military arrests during the rebellion, lose the right of public discussion, the liberty of speech and the press, the law of evidence, trial by jury, and Habeas corpus, throughout the indefinite peaceful future which I trust lies before them, any more than I am able to believe that a man could contract so strong an appetite for emetics during temporary illness, as to persist in feeding upon them through the remainder of his healthful life. . . .

A Painful Arrest

One of the resolutions expresses the opinion of the meeting that arbitrary arrests will have the effect to divide and distract those who should be united in suppressing the rebellion; and I am specifically called on to discharge Mr. Vallandigham. I regard this as, at least, a fair appeal to me, on the expediency of exercising a constitutional power which I think exists. In response to such appeal I have to say it gave me pain when I learned that Mr. V. had been arrested,— that is, I was pained that there should have seemed to be a necessity for arresting him—and that it will afford me great pleasure to discharge him so soon as I can, by any means, believe the public safety will not suffer by it. I further say, that as the war progresses, it appears to me, opinion, and action, which were in great confusion at first, take shape, and fall into more regular channels; so that the necessity for arbitrary [strong] dealing with them gradually decreases. I have every reason to desire that it would cease altogether, and far from the least is my regard for the opinions and wishes of those who, like the meeting at Albany, declare their purpose to sustain the government in every constitutional and lawful measure to suppress the rebellion. Still, I must continue to do so much as may seem to be required by the public safety.

Viewpoint 7

"The most remarkable feature of the campaign is perhaps that violence to property was accompanied by so little personal violence, and that homicide and rape were almost unknown."

Sherman's March to the Sea Was Not Barbaric

B.H. Liddell Hart

Captain Basil Henry Liddell Hart was one of the twentieth century's most prominent military historians and strategists. His theoretical writings on military maneuvers influenced both the German blitzkrieg (lightning war) and Allied general George S. Patton's tactics during the Battle of the Bulge during World War II.

Liddell Hart developed his most important ideas, which emphasized an army's mobility and use of surprise, while researching his 1929 biography of General William Tecumseh Sherman. Sherman's greatest military achievement was his March to the Sea during the last months of 1964. This march left a sixty-mile-wide swath of destruction through Georgia, cutting the Confederacy in half and crippling its ability to fight.

In popular legend, Sherman was a near-lunatic whose March

B.H. Liddell Hart, *Sherman: Soldier, Realist, American*. Boston: Dodd, Mead, 1929.

to the Sea was an act of unrestrained barbarity. But in Liddell Hart's view, Sherman was a brilliant and canny tactician whose violent language was seldom reflected in action. According to the following viewpoint, excerpted from Liddell Hart's biography of Sherman, the March to the Sea was remarkably restrained and orderly.

The army which marched with Sherman from Atlanta to the Atlantic was probably the finest army of military "workmen" the modern world has seen. An army of individuals trained in the school of experience to look after their own food and health, to march far and fast with the least fatigue, to fight with the least exposure; above all, to act swiftly and to work thoroughly. Each individual fitted into his place in a little group which, messing, marching and fighting together, by its instinctive yet intelligent teamship reduced alike the risks and the toil of the campaign. The sum of these teams formed an army of athletes stripped of all impediments, whether weight of kit or weaklings, and impelled by a sublime faith in their captain, "Uncle Billy," a faith which found vent in such slogans as "There goes the old man. All's right."

Goal of Mobility

Sherman's supreme aim in his preparations had been to develop the mobility of his army to such a pitch that it should be a huge "flying column" of light infantry. . . . The army, which finally totalled just over 60,000, was divided into a right wing . . . and a left wing. . . . Each corps was to be independent for supplies, to move on a separate road, and had a 900 feet section of the "wing" pontoon train [a line of connected, flat-bottom boats] given it. There was no general supply train and the corps supply trains were distributed among brigades, which in turn allotted one wagon only, for kit, and one ambulance to each regiment. In all there were about 2,500 wagons, each drawn by six mules, and 600 light ambulances. For mobility also each gun and caisson was drawn by an eight-horse team. Rations for twenty days and forage for five were carried, as well as two hundred rounds of ammunition per man and per gun, while each soldier marched out with forty rounds on his person and three days' rations in his haversack. Droves of beef-cattle accompanied the marching army. But while full precautions were taken to ensure comfortably filled stomachs, external comforts were pared down to little more than a blanket for each man, a coffee-pot and stewing pan for each group of messmates.

On this expedition Sherman fulfilled his ideal of mobility; setting a standard of fifteen miles for the daily march and allowing no comfort-loving subordinate to baulk him by laxness or lax example. The rations with which the army set out were to be treated as far as possible as a reserve, for the army was to live on the country. To this end each brigade organized a foraging party of thirty to fifty men under a picked officer. Every morning before daylight these would be off to scour the plantations several miles ahead, and out to the flanks, for livestock, corn and eatables of every kind. They would usually keep ahead of the column throughout the day, carrying each successive harvest, often on captured horses or carts, to the road along which the column was coming where it would be picked up by the supply trains. These foragers—Sherman's famous "bummers"—were commonly mounted on horses or mules taken from the plantations, and often ridden with a rope for rein and a strip of carpet for saddle.

A Game of War

Their utility did not end with their provisioning duties, for they automatically formed and intelligently acted as a wide screen of scouts covering the front and flanks of the marching column. Thereby they not only protected it from surprise, but saved it time-wasting deployments. If enemy cavalry appeared on the scene, the laden foragers would pour out of barns and kitchen gardens like a swarm of angry bees, each party rallying to form a well concealed and extended firing line, while some of their number drove the laden mules to the rear. If still pressed, they would make a fighting withdrawal while other parties converged to their support, and, being skilled in shooting and cover, constantly gave their opponents the impression that they were the main line of skirmishers. However careless of the forms of discipline, they were imbued with the essential fighting discipline, and developed such dashing team-work that they would clear the front of enemy cavalry quicker and better than the proper cavalry had done in the previous campaigns.

That team-work was all the better because it was treated as an exhilarating game rather than an enforced task—a game in which to score points and a "rag" [prank] in which to indulge humour. Into it they threw themselves with all the mingled enthusiasm and thoroughness of preparation which marks an undergraduate rag. And like all rags this, the greatest of all in scale and duration, was most exciting and amusing except for those who suffered by it.

A Robin Hood Touch

To the actual foraging no real limit was set, for, apart from the foraging parties, the orders liberally said that "soldiers . . . may be permitted to gather turnips, potatoes and other vegetables, and to drive in stock in sight of their camp." "As for horses, mules, wagons, etc., belonging to the inhabitants, the cavalry and artillery may appropriate freely and without limit, discriminating, however, between the rich, who are usually hostile, and the poor or industrious, usually neutral or friendly." A Robin Hood touch! The only restriction set was that "soldiers must not enter the dwellings of the inhabitants, or commit any trespass"—this clause kindles the vision of a forager using endearing blandishments to attract a reluctant pig from its sty to become pork. As to destruction, however, the limit was more strictly drawn—"To army corps commanders alone is intrusted the power to destroy mills, houses, cotton gins, etc., and for them this general principle is laid down: In districts . . . where the army is unmolested no destruction of such property should be permitted, but should guerrillas or bushwhackers molest our march, or should the inhabitants burn bridges, obstruct roads, or otherwise manifest local hostility, then army commanders should order and enforce a devastation more or less relentless according to the measure of such hostility."

Unavoidable Excesses

The elasticity of these limits in practice varied with the corps commander, and when a commander of [General Hugh Judson] Kilpatrick's wild temper and rapacious character had the deciding

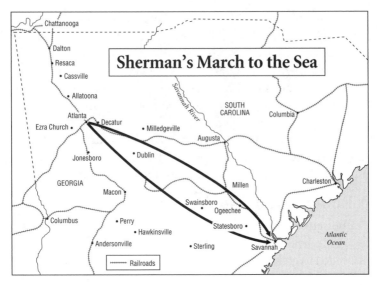

Sherman's March to the Sea

voice principles were often submerged in sheer lust of plunder and destruction. But power can be assumed, as well as entrusted, and in men trained to forage without limit the distinction between forage and pillage is easily obscured. And the pillager disappointed of detachable loot easily finds vent for his feelings in the destruction of fixtures, when the simple conjunction of a barn and a match can relieve them "brilliantly" at little risk of discovery.

That Sherman and many of his officers tried to check excesses and enforce limits is unquestionable. But the very width of front covered by the army on its march made supervision impossible, and even when culprits were detected the only punishment which could be an effective deterrent—death—could not be applied without specific sanction from Washington. All the men knew that Lincoln's mercy dropped ceaselessly like the gentle dew from heaven, and on this expedition had the further assurance that they were safely isolated from even the remote chance of a drought at Washington. Sherman, too, was handicapped by a conflict of principles in his own mind. On the one hand, filled with the idea that the war was at bedrock "a war *against anarchy*" he hated any and every act which savoured of illegality. On the other hand, this man, so kind and considerate as an individual, conceived himself as the angel of wrath, armed with a flaming sword, to punish a people guilty of a mortal sin—that of bringing division into the Union and hence of bringing war into the land.

A Full Reckoning

He himself, with some success, might reconcile the two principles in his actions, and intervene to check or frustrate many an abuse, but his words of violence carried further than his deeds. Among his staff were some whose attitude to the South was as passionate in its hatred as his attitude was dispassionate. [Lewis Mumford] Dayton, his inseparable aide-de-camp, and now his acting adjutant-general, was one. Some of them also had a genius for indiscretion, even if he himself had not been so carelessly generous in broadcasting his opinions and ebullitions. Thus it was natural that the idea should spread that Sherman himself favoured indiscriminate destruction, and that men as they ransacked a house of its edible property should laughingly quote to each other the words of his order—"Forage liberally on the country." The permanent damage wrought by the foraging parties or halted columns was comparatively slight however; the burning of barns and dwellings was usually the work of unauthorized foragers who, as the campaign progressed, extended both in space and time the radius of their light-hearted and light-fingered operations. Many of these were stragglers who followed in the wake or on the skirts of the army. That Sherman should be blamed for their crimes was an odd recoil from the vigour of his efforts, during three years of war, to suppress them and to induce the authorities to take drastic measures against this universal blot.

Yet, when the full reckoning is made, the most remarkable feature of the campaign is perhaps that violence to property was accompanied by so little personal violence, and that homicide and rape were almost unknown. In person, indeed, the citizens and women of the South suffered less than from their own defenders. Even Kilpatrick's cavalry were outrivalled by [Confederate general Joseph] Wheeler's, and the ruffianly behaviour of the latter caused many a cry to rise "save us from our friends." Nor were these outrages limited to the last hungry and desperate months of the campaign, for even during the first retreat to Atlanta Southern papers were complaining that "our own army, while falling back from Dalton, was even more dreaded by the inhabitants than was the army of Sherman.". . .

The Capture of Savannah

With the capture of Savannah the swath through Georgia was complete. The "granary of the South" had been ransacked, the Confederacy deprived of its essential resources—not only corn, but cotton, cattle, horses and mules; and 265 miles of railroad had been destroyed. Sherman calculated—if probably overcalculated—the damage in dollar values at $100,000,000, but the moral damage of having pierced the heart of the South, and of having demonstrated the inability of the Confederate armies to guard it, was incalculably greater. In the time-matured verdict of the Confederate general and historian [E.P.] Alexander—"There is no question that the moral effect of this march upon the country at large . . . was greater than would have been the most decided victory." No longer would the people of Georgia or of any neighbouring State credit the confident assurances of their leaders and press. To loss of faith the sequel is loss of hope and then, in turn, lack of "fight." It only remained to carry that impression into South Carolina and the fate of the Confederacy would be sealed. And this was the next stage of the great plan which had evolved in Sherman's mind.

Viewpoint 8

"Sherman was making war on the Southern mind. Clearly, revenge was part of Sherman's strategy."

Sherman's March to the Sea Was Driven by Vengeance

Jack Trammell

General William Tecumseh Sherman's tactics changed the rules of warfare, inspiring military commanders to destroy civilian infrastructure rather than kill enemy soldiers. The March to the Sea of 1864, which ripped a path of destruction across Georgia, was Sherman's most notorious use of this strategy. The march earned Sherman the undying hatred of Southerners and the undying admiration of military theorists. However much suffering Sherman inflicted, his tactics were long regarded as impeccable.

But recent historians and biographers have questioned this conventional wisdom. For example, Michael Fellman's biography *Citizen Sherman* portrays Sherman not as a military genius but as a near-psychotic bigot—a sexist and a racist who suffered from depression and paranoia. Indeed, Sherman's contemporaries often doubted his sanity. In the following viewpoint, the novelist, poet, and journalist Jack Trammell examines whether

Sherman's destructiveness was the result of strategic brilliance or an unbalanced mental state, whether his tactics were mentally sound, and whether his actions hastened or delayed the end of the war. Trammell concludes that Sherman was motivated at least in part by a desire for revenge. Trammell works for Randolph-Macon College in Ashland, Virginia.

U nion Gen. William Tecumseh Sherman always will be best remembered for his infamous March to the Sea in 1864.

"I can make . . . Georgia howl!" he said. "War is cruelty. There is no use trying to reform it. The crueler it is, the sooner it will be over." With studied patience, Sherman led his army of 62,000 seasoned veterans on a monthlong orgy of destruction through Georgia to the Atlantic Ocean, and then presented Savannah to President Lincoln as a "Christmas present."

Vilified by Southerners, viewed with indifference and even open hostility by many in the North, Sherman remains today an enigma.

Was he an unbalanced, untreated victim of recurrent depression, or was he a misunderstood military genius who invented modern warfare?

"He was the most remarkable combination of virtues and deficiencies produced in the high direction of the Union armies," historian Allan Nevins writes.

Contradictions

Sherman's career up to the battle for Atlanta typified the contradictions in his personality. Born in Ohio in 1820, he attended West Point through the influence of his stepfather, compiling so many demerits that he was nearly expelled, and yet he finished sixth in his class.

He spent 13 relatively successful years in the Army, and then failed miserably in several civilian enterprises. Before the war, he became the superintendent of the Louisiana State Seminary and Military Academy, forging close friendships with many future secessionists who would later become his bitter enemies.

When the war broke out, he turned down a Confederate commission and bravely led a Union regiment at the Battle of First Manassas. When he moved to Kentucky in the Western theater, however, he exhibited inexplicable anxiety and timidity, imagined spies behind every tree, lost sleep and weight, and was finally sent home by the Army to recuperate. He contemplated suicide.

An Army report led to stories in the press that he was insane, and were it not for his close friendship with Gen. Ulysses S. Grant, Sherman probably would never have been named to head the Federal Division of the Mississippi and to command of the Western Army when Grant left to confront Confederate Gen. Robert E. Lee in the East.

"He stood by me when I was crazy," Sherman later said of Grant. Lincoln also stood by him, perhaps recognizing a fellow victim of depression, telling Sherman before Shiloh through his wife that, "Your abilities would soon merit promotion."

Uncle Billy

Once in charge in the West, he immediately set out on a vigorous, logical course of action, surprising those who had grown accustomed to his apparent inconsistencies. He moved out from his base at Chattanooga and threatened northern Georgia and Atlanta.

It was during this time that his ideas about total warfare began to crystallize. The Southern people, he said, "Cannot be made to love us," but they "can be made to fear us." His leadership during this period was notably more confident and focused. His men began to call him "Uncle Billy."

They tempered their affection, however, with a latent degree of distrust. Sherman had long exhibited a tendency toward emotional and psychological irregularities dating back even before Kentucky, and his overall generalship during the Civil War cannot be examined without considering the impact of them.

A Psychological Terrorist

Many of the troubles stemmed from the death of his father when Sherman was 9 and the sometimes awkward relationship that evolved with his stepfather. He was not happy and regularly battled with his own feelings and insecurities. His correspondence with his wife, in addition to revealing a deep love of his children, also exposes a lurking sense of resentment, inadequacy and rejection that he would never fully escape, even when thrust into supreme leadership and hailed as the savior of the Union.

He would often view the starving, suffering children of Georgia with mixed emotions as he remembered his own children, safely at home.

"Captured houses and lands must be repeopled [sic] by Northern settlers," he wrote to his brother, Sen. John Sherman. Though never seriously contemplated by Washington authorities, Sherman's thoughts hint at the wild and unpredictable nature of his intellect.

"He was a psychological terrorist with a reputation for madness," biographer Michael Fellman says. "Always extreme," Mr. Nevins says.

But was he a great general?

Orderly and Sufficient

Sherman's original goal in Georgia was to prevent the Confederates from reinforcing Lee's forces in Virginia. Consequently, during spring 1864, he kept maximum pressure on Gen. Joseph Johnston and the Army of Tennessee, without seriously risking his own forces in major battle.

With the exception of Kennesaw Mountain [Georgia, June 27, 1864], where Sherman learned the same lesson about the cost of frontal assaults on fortified positions that Grant would learn at Cold Harbor [Virginia, June 3–12, 1864], Sherman's campaign leading up to the siege of Atlanta was orderly and sufficient, but far from aggressive, brilliant or complete.

Fortunately for Sherman, Johnston was replaced by Gen. John Bell Hood, whose overly ambitious counterattacks outside the perimeter defenses left the Confederate army wrecked, and the city doomed. The stubborn, grizzled general who entered Atlanta and began planning his next move was about to be transformed into a mythic hero larger than life not because of his military record to that point, but because of a dramatic strategic decision to make war on the civilian population of Georgia.

"His great military prestige is really based upon his visionary strategic and operational concepts," says Maj. Thomas Robisch in an article on the legalities of modern war. "Sherman is regarded as the first commander of the modern era."

Fear and Dread

The huge swath of Georgia that Sherman's army traveled through would be swept clean as if by a 60-mile-wide vacuum cleaner. He pored over census records so he could choose the wealthiest route in terms of agricultural production. His stated purpose was, "to make a hole in Georgia," and cripple the Confederacy by splitting it in two. In addition, he understood very well the psychological effect his march would have on the citizens. The Southern people could easily be "made to fear us, and dread the passage of troops through their country."

Proponents of "modern war" are quick to seize Sherman as their founding father, but his motives for the march remain less than crystal clear. He was no friend of blacks, saying, "All the Congresses on earth can't make the Negro anything else than what he is." He was, ironically, a Southern sympathizer before the war, and believed in the right to revolution. When secession became a reality, however, he was seized with anxiety, and spoke of a country that would be "drenched in blood." Later, his comments on those supporting the Confederate cause were often vitriolic.

Revenge may have been a primary motivator in Sherman's decision to punish Georgia. He considered secession a "crime against civilization," and did not hesitate to sever long friendships and associations with Southerners who supported the Confederacy. When asked about the burning of Columbia, S.C., after his army had turned north from Georgia, Sherman said: "I never shed many tears over the event."

Criminal Acts?

Lincoln and Grant initially opposed the idea of the march, and Sherman went to great lengths to promote it, even advocating it on the basis of the diplomatic benefits when military reasons alone were not enough to justify it: The world would witness the awesome power of the Union and the utter helplessness of the South.

Sherman's actions, however, belied his words, typified by the incident when he made his headquarters at the plantation of Gen.

Howell Cobb, a leading Rebel. "Spare nothing," he ordered, and everything was burned, despite the fact that the deserted plantation offered no significant material aid to the Confederacy.

According to Maj. Robisch, "Soldiers serving in the U.S. Army today would be criminally liable for larceny or destruction of property for similar conduct." It was hardly the kind of action that would engender international support.

What was the impact on the war, and on Georgia itself? Did Sherman's efforts at destruction of war materiel, industry, railroads and foodstuffs result in a tangible shortage for major Confederate armies in the field (such as Lee's), or did they merely result in short-term hardship for local citizens and militia?

The fact, mostly ignored for more than 137 years, is that Lee's army was defeated by Grant's tactical maneuvers, and not a lack of materiel. When the war closed, vast quantities of ammunition, clothing and food were still in warehouses in western North Carolina, and isolated parts of Virginia. Sherman's march did not destroy a fraction of the total goods manufactured in Richmond, for example.

As for Georgia, the local effect was more devastating. The march set the Georgia economy back for almost 100 years, and left deep psychological scars.

Strategy of Revenge

Would the war have ended sooner if Sherman had taken the course Grant did in Virginia, and pursued Hood's army to the death? No one can know, but it's certainly a reasonable possibility. Would peace have been made if Sherman hadn't embarked on the march, and Lincoln had been defeated in the election? This is a more difficult question, and has less to do with Sherman's personality and more to do with politics in the North.

Where Sherman's motives remain the most problematic are in regard to the punishment of the perpetrators of rebellion. Having worked and lived in the South, Sherman felt betrayed by those he had considered close friends and colleagues.

While he may have been sincere in his belief that "total war" would result in a quicker victory for the Union, the reality was that his erratic personality colored his command decisions, such as when he told the mayor of Atlanta: "Those who brought war into our country deserve all the curses and maledictions a people can pour out."

He went to enormous pains to justify his actions, even when they were clearly in violation of all formal and informal rules of warfare.

Biographer Lee Kennett refers to critic John C. Ropes, saying, "Sherman went beyond the attainment of purely military ends, applying devastation as a 'punishment for political conduct.'" Sherman was making war on the Southern mind. Clearly, revenge was part of Sherman's strategy.

After the war, Sherman once was asked and offered an answer to the same question: "What is strategy? Common sense applied to the art of war. You've got to do something. You can't go around asking corporals and sergeants. You must make it out in your own mind."

The Uses of Anger

The mind of Sherman was unpredictable and complex, and his decisions still remain controversial. Mr. Kennett, though, maintains it unlikely that he had more than a normal share of mental and behavioral problems. The words "depression" and "anxiety" appear nowhere in the index of Mr. Kennett's biography of Sherman, and there is little discussion of the "insanity" reported by Sherman's contemporaries.

Yet the allegations persist. A psychotherapist, Richard O'Conner, uses Sherman as an example of overcoming depression. "Sherman developed the ability to use . . . anger against his enemies, much to the dismay of Georgia."

One can certainly define Sherman by what he was not. He was not very well organized, nor was he an effective disciplinarian. For that matter, his tactical ability is suspect, as evidenced by his performances at Kennesaw Mountain (with its Cold Harbor–like casualties), Savannah (where he let Gen. William Hardee give him the slip) and Bentonville [North Carolina, March 19–20, 1865] (where he nearly let the entire wing of his army be destroyed).

His major tactical victory in high command was at Atlanta, where Hood did him the favor of impaling his Confederate Army of Tennessee on the Union defensive positions.

An Enigma

After the war, Sherman rose to command the entire army, and then became a popular speaker and commentator, but one who rarely referred to the famous march through Georgia, preferring instead to talk about the battles around Atlanta and other war topics. Yet the March to the Sea dominates his legacy, and the modern debates that center around him.

Impulsive, sometimes irrational and always restless, Sherman must remain an enigma, even to his apologists. In his own words, he summed up the kind of courage it took to lead on the battlefield, or to face psychological challenges: "A perfect sensibility of the measure of danger, and a willingness to endure it."

Sherman endures as both champion and villain.

CHAPTER 3

How Did the War End in a Union Victory?

Chapter Preface

Outgunned and outmanned though the Confederacy was, its war goals were fairly simple. It had to fend off a Northern invasion and preserve its independence. Strong as the Union was, its goals were more complex and troubling. It had to bring the Southern states back to the Union by force without further deepening national divisions.

When the war began, the Union's general in chief was Winfield Scott, a hero of the Mexican War of 1846–1848. Scott devised what became known as the Anaconda Plan. As its name suggests, the plan was to choke away the South's will to fight by the strategic placement of troops and naval blockades. Scott's intent was to end the rebellion with as little bloodshed and destruction as possible.

Although still mentally keen, Scott was too elderly to assume command. Besides, patience was needed for Scott's plan to work, and patience was in short supply. Hotter heads prevailed. "On to Richmond!" exclaimed the *New York Tribune*'s editor Horace Greeley. Bellicose fantasies of seizing the new Confederate capital led directly to a terrible Union defeat—the First Battle of Bull Run on July 21, 1861. From that day on, both North and South faced the reality of a long, bloody, destructive war.

Lincoln soon placed George B. McClellan in command of Union forces. Lincoln's quarrels with McClellan became the stuff of legend. McClellan did excellent work preparing the Union army and devising what seemed a workable plan to capture Richmond. But his reluctance to act gained him the nickname "Tardy George."

In fairness, McClellan's reluctance stemmed from concern for his troops and for the republic as a whole. He strongly believed that fighting the war too aggressively would render the Union irreparable. As he wrote to Lincoln,

> This rebellion has assumed the character of a War: as such it should be regarded; and it should be conducted upon the highest principles known to Christian Civilization. It should not be a War looking to the subjugation of the people of any

state, in any event. It should not be, at all, a War upon population; but against armed forces and political organizations. Neither confiscation of property, political executions of persons, territorial organization of states or forcible abolition of slavery should be contemplated for a moment.[1]

Unfortunately, this attitude proved inappropriate for waging the war. Time and time again, McClellan failed to seize strategic advantages. On September 17, 1862, McClellan's forces halted Robert E. Lee's invasion of Maryland at Antietam. "Our victory was complete," announced McClellan. "The enemy was driven back into Virginia."[2] McClellan sincerely believed that success meant pushing Lee's army back to Confederate territory. But in Lincoln's view, rebellious Virginia was as much a part of the Union as was loyal Maryland; there was really no such thing as Confederate territory. Lincoln here relates how McClellan let a final Union victory slip through his fingers:

> The Blue Ridge was then between our army and Lee's. I directed McClellan peremptorily to move on Richmond. It was eleven days before he crossed his first man over the Potomac; it was eleven days after that before he crossed the last man. Thus he was twenty-two days in passing the river at a much easier and more practicable ford than that where Lee crossed his entire army between dark one night and daylight the next morning. That was the last grain of sand which broke the camel's back. I relieved McClellan at once.[3]

Eventually, Lincoln found the generals he needed to fight such formidable Confederate leaders as James Longstreet and Robert E. Lee. These included Ulysses S. Grant, who became commander in chief of the Union forces on March 9, 1864, and William Tecumseh Sherman. Unlike their Southern counterparts, Grant and Sherman were far from glamorous, romantic figures. Grant was suspected (probably wrongly) of being a chronic drunk. Sherman was suspected (perhaps with reason) of being emotionally unstable. Nevertheless, they were excellent leaders and planners. They were also as complex and contradictory as their president and commander in chief, by turns compassionate and ruthless.

To be sure, the Union continued to suffer from faulty leadership. General George Meade defeated Confederate forces at the fateful Battle of Gettysburg of July 1–3, 1863. But like McClellan before him, Meade allowed Lee's forces to slip back across the Potomac, thus losing another chance for a final Union victory. But Grant, Sherman, and other Union officers quickly set to work attacking the South from every direction, restoring Winfield Scott's Anaconda Plan with a fearsome new emphasis. Instead of merely weakening the South as Scott had intended, Grant's more lethal strategy strangled the Confederacy to death.

The following chapter includes debates about the Union's progress during the Civil War.

Notes

1. George McClellan, letter to Abraham Lincoln, July 7, 1862.
2. George McClellan, letter to H.W. Halleck, September 19, 1862.
3. Abraham Lincoln, discussion with journalists, March 1863.

Viewpoint 1

"After four years of failure to restore the Union by the experiment of war, . . . justice, humanity, liberty, and the public welfare demand that immediate efforts be made for a cessation of hostilities."

The War Has Been a Union Failure

Democratic Party

The Democratic convention met in Chicago on August 29, 1864. The Democrats chose as their presidential candidate George B. McClellan, whom Lincoln had earlier dismissed as general in chief of the Union forces. With good reason, the Democrats were confident of winning the presidency in November on an antiwar platform. Lincoln's popularity was low, and the Union was demoralized by recent military setbacks, including the near-capture of Washington by Confederate forces in July. Lincoln himself acknowledged that "it seems exceedingly probable that this administration will not be reelected."

The 1864 Democratic Party Platform, presented here in its entirety, sharply criticized not only the war itself, but many of Lincoln's wartime policies. Although the platform did not specifically mention the Emancipation Proclamation of January 1863, it was implicitly criticized. Lincoln's proclamation had turned the war into a crusade against slavery. In the eyes of the Demo-

Democratic Party, *Democratic Party Platform*, 1864.

crats, this turn of events made the South's peaceful return to the Union impossible. The platform's complete avoidance of the word *slavery* made a subtle but crucial point: Abolition was out of the question.

R esolved, That in the future, as in the past, we will adhere with unswerving fidelity to the Union under the Constitution as the only solid foundation of our strength, security, and happiness as a people, and as a framework of government equally conducive to the welfare and prosperity of all the States, both Northern and Southern.

The Government Has Ignored the Constitution

Resolved, That this convention does explicitly declare, as the sense of the American people, that after four years of failure to restore the Union by the experiment of war, during which, under the pretense of a military necessity of war-power higher than the Constitution, the Constitution itself has been disregarded in every part, and public liberty and private right alike trodden down, and the material prosperity of the country essentially impaired, justice, humanity, liberty, and the public welfare demand that immediate efforts be made for a cessation of hostilities, with a view of an ultimate convention of the States, or other peaceable means, to the end that, at the earliest practicable moment, peace may be restored on the basis of the Federal Union of the States.

Resolved, That the direct interference of the military authorities of the United States in the recent elections held in Kentucky, Maryland, Missouri, and Delaware was a shameful violation of the Constitution, and a repetition of such acts in the approaching election will be held as revolutionary, and resisted with all the means and power under our control.

The Aim Is to Preserve the Constitution

Resolved, That the aim and object of the Democratic party is to preserve the Federal Union and the rights of the States unimpaired, and they hereby declare that they consider that the administrative usurpation of extraordinary and dangerous powers not granted by the Constitution—the subversion of the civil by military law in States not in insurrection; the arbitrary military arrest, imprisonment, trial, and sentence of American citizens in States where civil law exists in full force; the suppression of freedom of speech and of the press; the denial of the right of asylum; the open and avowed disregard of State rights; the employment of unusual test-oaths; and the interference with and denial of the right of the people to bear arms in their defense—is calculated to prevent a restoration of the Union and the perpetuation of a Government deriving its just powers from the consent of the governed.

The Citizens Have Been Prisoners of War

Resolved, That the shameful disregard of the Administration to its duty in respect to our fellow citizens who now are and long have been prisoners of war and in a suffering condition, deserves the severest reprobation on the score alike of public policy and common humanity.

Resolved, That the sympathy of the Democratic party is heartily and earnestly extended to the soldiery of our army and sailors of our navy, who are and have been in the field and on the sea under the flag of our country, and, in the events of its attaining power, they will receive all the care, protection, and regard that the brave soldiers and sailors of the republic have so nobly earned.

Viewpoint 2

"The important fact remains demonstrated, that we have more *men* now *than we had when the war* began; *that we are not exhausted, nor in process of exhaustion; that we are* gaining *strength."*

The War Has Been a Union Success

Abraham Lincoln

Hardly had the Democrats written their 1864 platform declaring the Union war effort a failure when General William Tecumseh Sherman captured Atlanta, Georgia. He soon began his notorious March to the Sea, cutting a great swath of destruction through Georgia and crippling the South's ability to fight. By the time of the November 1864 election, the war hardly seemed the Union failure condemned in the Democratic platform. Abraham Lincoln was reelected by 55 percent of the popular vote, and Republicans increased their majority in Congress.

Lincoln was elected on a Republican platform that cited slavery as the cause of the Civil War and called for a constitutional amendment ending slavery. Such an amendment had been proposed in April of that year but had failed to carry the two-thirds majority required in the House of Representatives. On December 6, Lincoln trumpeted the Union's successes in his annual message to Congress, from which the following viewpoint is ex-

Abraham Lincoln, annual address to the U.S. Congress, Washington, DC, December 6, 1864.

cerpted. By then, Lincoln felt confident that the antislavery amendment would soon pass. The Thirteenth Amendment did pass quickly in Congress, but it was not legally adopted until December 6, 1865—after Lincoln's assassination.

Lincoln's Annual Message to Congress, 1864

The war continues. Since the last annual message all the important lines and positions then occupied by our forces have been maintained, and our arms have steadily advanced; thus liberating the regions left in rear, so that Missouri, Kentucky, Tennessee and parts of other States have again produced reasonably fair crops.

The Signs of Our Success

The most remarkable feature in the military operations of the year is General Sherman's attempted march of three hundred miles directly through the insurgent region. It tends to show a great increase of our relative strength that our General-in-Chief should feel able to confront and hold in check every active force of the enemy, and yet to detach a well-appointed large army to move on such an expedition. The result not yet being known, conjecture in regard to it is not here indulged.

Important movements have also occurred during the year to the effect of moulding society for durability in the Union. Although short of complete success, it is much in the right direction, that twelve thousand citizens in each of the States of Arkansas and Louisiana have organized loyal State governments with free constitutions, and are earnestly struggling to maintain and administer them. The movements in the same direction, more extensive, though less definite in Missouri, Kentucky and Tennessee, should not be overlooked. But Maryland presents the example of complete success. Maryland is secure to Liberty and Union for all the future. The genius of rebellion will no more claim Maryland. Like another foul spirit, being driven out, it may seek to tear her, but it will woo her no more.

Public Opinion Supports Us

At the last session of Congress a proposed amendment of the Constitution abolishing slavery throughout the United States, passed the Senate, but failed for lack of the requisite two-thirds vote in the House of Representatives. Although the present is the same Congress, and nearly the same members, and without questioning the wisdom or patriotism of those who stood in opposition, I venture to recommend the reconsideration and passage of the measure at the present session. Of course the abstract question is not changed; but an intervening election shows, almost certainly, that the next Congress will pass the measure if this does not. Hence there is only a question of *time* as to when the proposed amendment will go to the States for their action. And as it is to so go, at all events, may we not agree that the sooner the better? It is not claimed that the election has imposed a duty on members to change their views or their votes, any further than, as an additional element to be considered, their judgment may be affected by it. It is the voice of the people now, for the first time, heard upon the question. In a great national crisis, like ours, unanimity of action among those seeking a common end is very desirable—almost indispensable. And yet no approach to such unanimity is attainable, unless some deference shall be paid to the will of the majority, simply because it is the will of the majority. In this case the common end is the maintenance of the Union; and, among the means to secure that end, such will, through the election, is most clearly declared in favor of such constitutional amendment.

The most reliable indication of public purpose in this country is derived through our popular elections. Judging by the recent canvass and its result, the purpose of the people, within the loyal States, to maintain the integrity of the Union, was never more firm, nor more nearly unanimous, than now. The extraordinary calmness and good order with which the millions of voters met and mingled at the polls, give strong assurance of this. Not only all those who supported the Union ticket, so called, but a great majority of the opposing party also, may be fairly claimed to entertain, and to be actuated by, the same purpose. It is an unanswerable argument to this effect, that no candidate for any office whatever, high or low, has ventured to seek votes on the avowal that he was for giving up the Union. There have been much impugning of motives, and much heated controversy as to the proper means and best mode of advancing the Union cause; but

"The Almighty Has His Own Purposes"

On March 4, 1865, about three months after his annual message to Congress, Lincoln delivered his much more somber second inaugural address, excerpted below. In it, Lincoln suggests that the war has been wrought by God in order to bring an end to slavery.

Both [sides] read the same Bible, and pray to the same God; and each invokes His aid against the other. . . . The prayers of both could not be answered; that of neither has been answered fully. The Almighty has His own purposes. "Woe unto the world because of offences! for it must needs be that offences come; but woe to that man by whom the offence cometh!" If we shall suppose that American Slavery is one of those offences which, in the providence of God, must needs come, but which, having continued through His appointed time, He now wills to remove, and that He gives to both North and South, this terrible war, as the woe due to those by whom the offence came, shall we discern therein any departure from those divine attributes which the believers in a Living God always ascribe to Him? Fondly do we hope—fervently do we pray—that this mighty scourge of war may speedily pass away. Yet, if God wills that it continue, until all the wealth piled by the bond-man's two hundred and fifty years of unrequited toil shall be sunk, and until every drop of blood drawn with the lash, shall be paid by another drawn with the sword, as was said three thousand years ago, so still it must be said "the judgments of the Lord, are true and righteous altogether."

Abraham Lincoln, second inaugural address, March 4, 1865.

on the distinct issue of Union or no Union, the politicians have shown their instinctive knowledge that there is no diversity among the people. In affording the people the fair opportunity of showing, one to another and to the world, this firmness and unanimity of purpose, the election has been of vast value to the national cause.

We Are Gaining Strength and Resources

The election has exhibited another fact not less valuable to be known—the fact that we do not approach exhaustion in the most important branch of national resources—that of living men. While it is melancholy to reflect that the war has filled so many graves, and carried mourning to so many hearts, it is some relief to know that, compared with the surviving, the fallen have been so few. While corps, and divisions, and brigades, and regiments have formed, and fought, and dwindled, and gone out of existence, a great majority of the men who composed them are still living. The same is true of the naval service. The election returns prove this. So many voters could not else be found. . . .

Thousands, white and black, join us as the national arms press back the insurgent lines. So much is shown, affirmatively and negatively, by the election. It is not material to inquire *how* the increase has been produced, or to show that it would have been *greater* but for the war, which is probably true. The important fact remains demonstrated, that we have *more* men *now* than we had when the war *began;* that we are not exhausted, nor in process of exhaustion; that we are *gaining* strength, and may, if need be, maintain the contest indefinitely. This as to men. Material resources are now more complete and abundant than ever.

The national resources, then, are unexhausted, and, as we believe, inexhaustible. The public purpose to reestablish and maintain the national authority is unchanged, and, as we believe, unchangeable. The manner of continuing the effort remains to choose. On careful consideration of all the evidence accessible it seems to me that no attempt at negotiation with the insurgent leader [President Jefferson Davis] could result in any good. He would accept nothing short of severance of the Union—precisely what we will not and cannot give. His declarations to this effect are explicit and oft-repeated. He does not attempt to deceive us. He affords us no excuse to deceive ourselves. He cannot voluntarily reaccept the Union; we cannot voluntarily yield it. Between him and us the issue is distinct, simple, and inflexible. It is an issue which can only be tried by war, and decided by victory. If we yield, we are beaten; if the Southern people fail him, he is beaten. Either way, it would be the victory and defeat following war. What is true, however, of him who heads the insurgent cause, is not necessarily true of those who follow. Although he cannot reaccept the Union, they can. Some of them, we know, already desire peace and reunion. The number of such may increase. They can, at any moment, have peace simply by laying down their arms and submitting to the national authority under the Constitution.

Viewpoint 3

"Operating in the interior of our own country . . . nothing is now needed to render our triumph certain but the exhibition of our own unquenchable resolve."

The South Should Never Surrender

Jefferson Davis

Jefferson Davis, the first and only president of the Confederate States of America, is generally remembered by historians as an able but flawed leader. Against seemingly impossible odds, he managed to hold a deeply divided government together during four years of terrible war. But he could be dictatorial, thin-skinned, and heedless of the advice of others, and his judgment sometimes failed him. Perhaps his greatest error was in defending the Confederate capital of Richmond, Virginia, at all costs, neglecting more pressing military concerns elsewhere.

On April 3, 1865, Davis was forced to abandon Richmond, and Union troops occupied the city. The following viewpoint is Davis's last presidential address, delivered the day after Richmond's capture. Here Davis gives way to self-deception, refusing to acknowledge the hopelessness of the Confederate situation and insisting on continuing the war with guerrilla tactics.

On April 9, a mere five days after Davis's address, Confederate general Robert E. Lee formally surrendered to Union general

Jefferson Davis, presidential address to the people of the Confederacy, April 4, 1865.

Ulysses S. Grant at the town of Appomattox Court House, Virginia, effectively ending the Civil War. Even then, Jefferson Davis refused to surrender. Captured in Georgia on May 10, 1865, he was imprisoned for two years, but he was never tried for treason. He died in New Orleans in 1889.

To the People of the Confederate States of America:

The general in chief of our army has found it necessary to make such movements of the troops as to uncover the capital and thus involve the withdrawal of the government from the city of Richmond.

It would be unwise, even were it possible, to conceal the great moral as well as material injury to our cause that must result from the occupation of Richmond by the enemy. It is equally unwise and unworthy of us, as patriots engaged in a most sacred cause, to allow our energies to falter, our spirits to grow faint, or our efforts to become relaxed under reverses, however calamitous. While it has been to us a source of national pride that for four years of unequaled warfare we have been able, in close proximity to the center of the enemy's power, to maintain the seat of our chosen government free from the pollution of his presence; while the memories of the heroic dead who have freely given their lives to its defense must ever remain enshrined in our hearts; while the preservation of the capital, which is usually regarded as the evidence to mankind of separate existence, was an object very dear to us, it is also true, and should not be forgotten, that the loss which we have suffered is not without compensation.

For many months the largest and finest army of the Confederacy, under the command of a leader whose presence inspires equal confidence in the troops and the people, has been greatly trammeled by the necessity of keeping constant watch over the approaches to the capital, and has thus been forced to forego more than one opportunity for promising enterprises.

Encounter Danger with Courage

The hopes and confidence of the enemy have been constantly excited by the belief that their possession of Richmond would be the signal for our submission to their rule and relieve them from the burden of war which, as their failing resources admonish them, must be abandoned if not speedily brought to a successful close.

It is for us, my countrymen, to show by our bearing under reverses how wretched has been the self-deception of those who have believed us less able to endure misfortune with fortitude than to encounter danger with courage.

We have now entered upon a new phase of a struggle the memory of which is to endure for all ages and to shed ever increasing luster upon our country. Relieved from the necessity of guarding cities and particular points, important but not vital to our defense, with our army free to move from point to point and strike in detail the detachments and garrisons of the enemy; operating in the interior of our own country, where supplies are more accessible and where the foe will be far removed from his own base and cut off from all succor in case of reverse, nothing is now needed to render our triumph certain but the exhibition of our own unquenchable resolve. Let us but will it, and we are free; and who, in the light of the past, dare doubt your purpose in the future?

No Peace with Invaders

Animated by that confidence in your spirit and fortitude, which never yet has failed me, I announce to you, fellow countrymen, that it is my purpose to maintain your cause with my whole heart and soul; that I will never consent to abandon to the enemy one foot of the soil of any one of the states of the Confederacy; that Virginia, noble state, whose ancient renown has [been] eclipsed by her still more glorious recent history; whose bosom has been bared to receive the main shock of this war; whose sons and daughters have exhibited heroism so sublime as to render her illustrious in all time to come; that Virginia, with the help of the people and by the blessing of Providence, shall be held and defended, and no peace ever be made with the infamous invaders of her homes by the sacrifice of any of her rights or territory.

If by stress of numbers we should ever be compelled to a temporary withdrawal from her limits, or those of any other border state, again and again will we return, until the baffled and exhausted enemy shall abandon in despair his endless and impossible task of making slaves of a people resolved to be free.

Let us not then despond, my countrymen, but, relying on the never failing mercies and protecting care of our God, let us meet the foe with fresh defiance, with unconquered and unconquerable hearts.

Viewpoint 4

"A partisan war may be continued . . . causing individual suffering and the devastation of the country, but I see no prospect by that means of achieving a separate independence."

The South Should Cease Fighting

Robert E. Lee

Robert E. Lee remains the Confederacy's most charismatic and fascinating figure. After loyal service in the U.S. Army for thirty-six years, Lee was troubled when Abraham Lincoln offered him command of Union forces on the eve of the Civil War. Although Lee opposed secession, his loyalty to his home state of Virginia prevailed over his loyalty to the Union, and he joined the Confederate cause. He served brilliantly as commander of the Army of Northern Virginia before taking command of all Southern armies in February 1865.

By the middle of 1864, however, even Lee's military genius could not save the Confederacy from overwhelming Union forces led by General Ulysses S. Grant. On April 9, 1865, Lee surrendered to Grant at Appomattox Court House, Virginia. Although some fighting continued afterward, historians recognize this date as the end of the Civil War. The following viewpoint is Lee's final letter to President Jefferson Davis, describing the demoralized condition of Confederate soldiers and recom-

Robert E. Lee, letter to Jefferson Davis, April 20, 1865.

mending that Davis take measures to end the war. Lee's appeal was futile; Davis refused to surrender until his own capture on May 10, 1865.

After the war, Lee became president of Washington College (later Washington and Lee University) in Lexington, Virginia, a position he held until his death in 1870.

M r. President:
The apprehensions I expressed during the winter, of the moral condition of the Army of Northern Virginia, have been realized. The operations which occurred while the troops were in the entrenchments in front of Richmond and Petersburg were not marked by the boldness and decision which formerly characterized them. Except in particular instances, they were feeble; and a want of confidence seemed to possess officers and men. This condition, I think, was produced by the state of feeling in the country, and the communications received by the men from their homes, urging their return and the abandonment of the field. The movement of the enemy on the 30th March to Dinwiddie [Virginia] Court House was consequently not as strongly met as similar ones had been. Advantages were gained by him which discouraged the troops, so that on the morning of the 2d April, when our lines between the Appomattox and Hatcher's Run were assaulted, the resistance was not effectual: several points were penetrated and large captures made. At the commencement of the withdrawal of the army from the lines on the night of the 2d, it began to disintegrate, and straggling from the ranks increased up to the surrender on the 9th.

The Spirit of Surrender

On that day, as previously reported, there were only seven thousand eight hundred and ninety-two (7892) effective infantry. During the night, when the surrender became known, more than ten thousand men came in, as reported to me by the Chief Commissary of the Army. During the succeeding days stragglers continued to give themselves up, so that on the 12th April, according to the rolls of those paroled, twenty-six thousand and eighteen (26,018) officers and men had surrendered. Men who had left the ranks on the march, and crossed James River, returned and gave themselves up, and many have since come to Richmond and sur-

A Fond Farewell

The day after his surrender at Appomattox Court House, General Robert E. Lee issued this touching farewell to the troops. He was perhaps showing characteristic gallantry in assuring his men that he had "no distrust of them"; by the last days of the war, Confederate troops were deserting in astonishing numbers.

After four years of arduous service marked by unsurpassed courage and fortitude, the Army of Northern Virginia has been compelled to yield to overwhelming numbers and resources.

I need not tell the survivors of so many hard-fought battles who have remained steadfast to the last that I have consented to this result from no distrust of them; but feeling that valor and devotion could accomplish nothing that would compensate for the loss that must have attended the continuance of the contest, I determined to avoid the useless sacrifice of those whose past services have endeared them to their countrymen. By the terms of the agreement, officers and men can return to their homes and remain until exchanged.

You may take with you the satisfaction that proceeds from the consciousness of duty faithfully performed, and I earnestly pray that a merciful God will extend to you His blessing and protection.

With an unceasing admiration of your constancy and devotion to your country, and a grateful remembrance of your kind and generous consideration of myself, I bid you all an affectionate farewell.

Robert E. Lee, farewell to the troops, April 10, 1865.

rendered. I have given these details that Your Excellency might know the state of feeling which existed in the army, and judge of that in the country. From what I have seen and learned, I believe an army cannot be organized or supported in Virginia, and as far as I know the condition of affairs, the country east of the Mississippi is morally and physically unable to maintain the contest unaided with any hope of ultimate success. A partisan war may be continued, and hostilities protracted, causing individual suffering and the devastation of the country, but I see no prospect by that means of achieving a separate independence. It is for Your Excellency to decide, should you agree with me in opinion, what is proper to be done. To save useless effusion of blood, I would recommend measures be taken for suspension of hostilities and the restoration of peace.

I am with great respect, yr obdt svt

R.E. Lee

Genl

Viewpoint 5

"In September 1862, the Confederacy appeared to be on the brink of victory. Antietam shattered that momentum."

Antietam Marked the Turning Point of the War

James M. McPherson

James M. McPherson is perhaps the most esteemed living scholar of the Civil War and Reconstruction. He won the 1988 Pulitzer Prize for *Battle Cry of Freedom*. His 2002 book *Crossroads of Freedom: Antietam*, from which the following viewpoint is taken, deals with the bloodiest single day in American history.

In September 1862, Confederate general Robert E. Lee led his troops into Maryland, threatening Washington, D.C. On September 17, Lee's forces met those of Union general George B. McClellan at Antietam Creek near Sharpsburg, Maryland. McClellan drove Lee back into Virginia in a terrible battle that killed thousands of men on both sides. The Battle of Antietam (or the Battle of Sharpsburg, as it is known in the South) was hardly a decisive military victory; McClellan's refusal to pursue Lee's army afterward almost certainly prolonged the war. Nevertheless, much changed after Antietam. Great Britain suddenly

146

felt reluctant to recognize and assist the Confederacy. Moreover, Lincoln seized the victory as an opportunity to issue his preliminary Emancipation Proclamation of September 22, followed by the full Emancipation Proclamation of January 1, 1863. These documents helped transform the Civil War into a crusade against slavery.

In this viewpoint, McPherson describes Antietam's horrible aftermath and proposes that the battle marked the turning point of the Civil War. Although the Confederacy had subsequent successes, it never regained the momentum it had achieved before Antietam.

Despite the ghastly events of September 11, 2001, another September day 139 years earlier remains the bloodiest single day in American history. The 6,300 to 6,500 Union and Confederate soldiers killed and mortally wounded near the Maryland village of Sharpsburg on September 17, 1862, were more than twice the number of fatalities suffered in the terrorist attacks on the World Trade Center and the Pentagon on September 11, 2001. Another 15,000 men wounded in the battle of Antietam would recover, but many of them would never again walk on two legs or work with two arms. The number of casualties at Antietam was four times greater than American casualties at the Normandy beaches on June 6, 1944. More American soldiers died at Sharpsburg (the Confederate name for the battle) than died in combat in all the other wars fought by this country in the nineteenth century *combined:* the War of 1812, the Mexican-American War, the Spanish-American War, and all the Indian wars.

The Dead and Wounded

Even at the distance of 140 years, such statistics send a shiver down one's spine. Yet these cold facts pale in comparison with descriptions of the battlefield by participants and witnesses—mainly Northerners, because the Confederate Army of Northern Virginia retreated across the Potomac River on the night of September 18–19, leaving most of their dead and many wounded to be buried or treated by the Union Army of the Potomac. "I was on the battlefield yesterday where we were engaged," wrote a Union artillery officer on September 19, "and the dead rebels strewed the ground and in some places were on top of each other. Two hundred dead could be counted in one small field." Another Northern officer counted "hundreds of dead bodies lying in rows and in piles . . . looking the picture of all that is sickening, harrowing, horrible. O what a terrible sight!" A Union lieutenant in charge of a burial party where his regiment (57th New York) fought described the dead "in every state of mutilation, sans [without] arms, sans legs, heads, and intestines, and in greater number than on any field we have seen before." A local resident who rode over the battlefield on September 19 traced the Confederate line "by the dead lying along it as they fell. . . . The line I suppose was a mile long or more. . . . Down in the corn field I saw a man with a hole in his belly about as big as a hat and about a quart of dark-looking maggots working away."

The most concentrated carnage took place in a sunken farm road in the center of the Confederate line, known ever after as Bloody Lane. A Union lieutenant colonel whose New York regiment was in the thick of the fighting at Bloody Lane described the scene there after the battle: "In the road the dead covered the ground. It seemed, as I rode along, that it was the Valley of Death. I think that in the space of less than ten acres, lay the bodies of a thousand dead men and as many more wounded." An enlisted man in this regiment who had captured a Confederate battle flag in the sunken road wrote in his diary on September 19: "Today I was given detaile to burry the Dead Rebels, just where I captured the flag at 2:00 PM of the 17th. 12 lengths of fence being counted off for my station & in 10 rods [55 yards] we have piled and burried 264 . . . & 4 Detailes has been obliged to do likewise, it was a Sight I never want to encounter again." A lieutenant in the 14th Connecticut, which also fought at Bloody Lane, described "hundreds of horses too, all mangled and putrefying, scattered everywhere."

A Scene from Hell

By September 24 the bodies were buried and some of the horses had been dragged into piles, doused with coal oil, and burned. But the battlefield still presented a scene from hell, as described by an

official of the United States Sanitary Commission who had
brought medical supplies for the wounded. "No words can con-
vey" the "utter devastation and ruin," he wrote, but he tried to
find words anyway. "For four miles in length, and nearly half a
mile in width, the ground is strewn with . . . hats, caps, clothing,
canteens, knapsacks, shells and shot." Scattered around were "long
mounds of earth, where, underneath, five thousand men, wrapped
in their blankets, were laid side by side. . . . Visit a battlefield and
see what a victory costs!"

A week after the battle a newspaper in Hagerstown (a dozen
miles from the battlefield) reported that in an area of seventy-five
square miles "wounded and dying soldiers are to be found in every neighborhood and in nearly every house. . . . The whole region
of country between Boonsboro and Sharpsburg is one vast hos-
pital" and "nearly the whole population" were trying to take care
of the wounded. This was no pleasant task. "The odor from the
battlefield and the hospitals is almost insupportable," wrote the

*A costly victory at Antietam, followed by the Emancipation Proclamation,
turned the Civil War in favor of the Union.*

surgeon of a New Hampshire regiment. "No one can begin to estimate the amount of agony after a great battle. . . . The poor mutilated soldiers that yet have life and sensation make a most horrid picture."

Months after the battle, Sharpsburg continued to disgorge new forms of hideousness. During Robert E. Lee's invasion of Pennsylvania in June 1863, which culminated in the battle of Gettysburg, part of his army marched over the Antietam battlefield. A private in the 23rd Virginia described "the most horrible sights that my eyes ever beheld," hundreds of bodies that had been buried in shallow graves the previous September "just lying on top of the ground with a little dirt throwed over them and the hogs rooting them out of the ground and eating them and others lying on top of the ground with the flesh picked off and their bones bleaching."

The War's Worst Battle

Major Rufus Dawes of the 6th Wisconsin, a regiment in the famous Iron Brigade, fought through the war in most of the Eastern theater's deadliest battles: Second Bull Run, Fredericksburg, Gettysburg, the Wilderness, Spotsylvania, and the battles around Petersburg as well as at Antietam. Looking back after the war, he wrote that Antietam "surpassed all in manifest evidence of slaughter." Many other veterans on both sides echoed this conclusion. A survey of thousands of surviving Union and Confederate soldiers after the war found that for an extraordinary number of them, no matter how many other battles they had fought, Antietam stood out as the worst.

Stark memories of Antietam haunted many for the rest of their days. A private in the 1st Delaware, which suffered 230 casualties in the battle, recalled a Union soldier "stumbling around with both eyes shot out, begging someone 'for the love of God' to put an end to his misery." A nearby lieutenant asked him if he really meant what he said. "Oh yes," the blinded soldier replied. "I cannot possibly live, and my agony is unendurable." Without another word the lieutenant drew his revolver, "placed it to the victim's right ear, turned away his head, and pulled the trigger. A half-wheel, a convulsive gasp, and one more unfortunate had passed over to the silent majority. 'It was better thus,' said the lieutenant, replacing his pistol and turning toward [me], 'for the poor fellow could—' Just then a solid shot took the lieutenant's head off."

Words Fail

The shock of such scenes caused psychiatric casualties among even the most hardened and experienced soldiers. Colonel William R. Lee of the elite 20th Massachusetts, who had gone through a half-dozen previous battles without losing his poise, rode away from his regiment the morning after Antietam without telling anyone and was later found, according to one of his subordinates, "without a cent in his pocket, without anything to eat or drink, without having changed his clothes for 4 weeks, during all which time he had this horrible diarrhea. . . . He was just like a little child wandering away from home."

Soldiers who wrote home to family members eager to hear about their experiences told them that they could not begin to depict the enormity of it. "Words are inadequate to portray the scene," wrote one. "I will not attempt to tell you of it," inscribed another. For Northern civilians who wanted to see something of the "ghastly spectacle" without actually going there, an opportunity soon presented itself. Within two days of the battle, Northern photographers Alexander Gardner and James Gibson arrived at Antietam and began taking pictures. For the first time in history, the graphic and grisly sight of bloated corpses killed in action could be seen by those who never came close to the battlefield. Gardner and Gibson worked for Mathew Brady, whose studio in New York City exhibited the photographs a month after the battle.

Photographic Eloquence

The unburied soldiers in these photographs were nearly all Confederates—probably because the Union dead were interred first, before Gardner and Gibson arrived, but perhaps also because pictures of Union dead might have had a dampening effect on Northern morale. In any event, a *New York Times* reporter who saw this exhibit on "The Dead of Antietam" wrote sympathetically of their Southern families whose grief invited empathy rather than enmity. "Mr. Brady has done something to bring home to us the terrible reality and earnestness of war," he informed readers of the *Times* on October 20, 1862. "If he has not brought bodies and laid them in our door-yards and along streets, he has done something very like it." But "there is one side of the picture that . . . has escaped photographic skill. It is the background of widows and orphans. . . . Homes have been made desolate, and the light of life in thousands of hearts has been quenched forever. All of this desolation imagination must paint—broken hearts cannot be photographed."

What had been accomplished by "all of this desolation"? The surgeon of a New Hampshire regiment, who remained in the vicinity of Sharpsburg for more than a month to treat the wounded, could find no answer to this question. "To the feeling man this war is truly a tragedy but to the thinking man it must appear a *madness*," he wrote. "We win a great victory. It goes through the country. The masses rejoice, but if all could see the thousands of poor, suffering, dieing men their rejoicing would turn to weeping. . . . ! pray God may stop such infernal work— though perhaps he has sent it upon us for our sins. Great indeed must have been our sins if such is our punishment."

A Massachusetts officer who fought at Antietam also was troubled to fathom its meaning. Robert Gould Shaw was a captain in the 2nd Massachusetts Infantry, one of the best Union regiments on the field. "Every battle makes me wish more and more that the war was over," Shaw wrote to his father four days after the carnage. "It seems almost as if nothing could justify a battle like that of the 17th, and the horrors inseparable from it."

Shaw's next battle was the assault on Fort Wagner on July 18, 1863, in which he was killed at the head of the 54th Massachusetts, the first black regiment recruited in the North. His family believed that the courage Shaw and his men demonstrated in that battle justified his death. But Shaw's question about Antietam lingers; what could justify such slaughter and desolation as occurred there? Two men who would have agreed on little else answered that question in a similar way. From London, where he followed the American Civil War with close attention, Karl Marx wrote in October 1862 that Antietam "has decided the fate of the American Civil War." And looking back some years later, Colonel Walter H. Taylor of Robert E. Lee's wartime staff described Sharpsburg as the decisive "event of the war."

The Fateful Event

Many soldiers who fought there would have agreed that Antietam was "the event" that decided "the fate of the American Civil War." They believed that the destiny of their respective nations—the United States and the Confederate States—rested on the outcome of this battle. They fought as if there would be no tomorrow. That was why for so many of them there *was* no tomorrow. For the others, of course, there were many more tomorrows and much more bloodshed as the war continued for two and one-half years after Antietam.

No single battle decided the outcome of the Civil War. Several turning points brought reversals of an apparently inexorable momentum toward victory by one side and then the other during the war. Two such pivotal moments occurred in the year that preceded Antietam. Union naval and military victories in the early months of 1862 blunted previous Southern triumphs and brought the Confederacy almost to its knees. But Southern counteroffensives in the summer turned the war around. When the Army of Northern Virginia crossed the Potomac River into Maryland in September 1862, the Confederacy appeared to be on the brink of victory. Antietam shattered that momentum. Never again did Southern armies come so close to conquering a peace for an independent Confederacy as they did in September 1862. Even though the war continued and the Confederacy again approached success on later occasions. Antietam was arguably, as Karl Marx and Walter Taylor believed, *the* event of the war.

"The Civil War is, to most Americans, what Lincoln wanted it to mean. Words had to complete the work of the guns."

Lincoln's Gettysburg Address Marked the Turning Point of the Civil War

Garry Wills

One of America's most wide-ranging intellectuals, author Garry Wills has made forays into biography (*John Wayne's America*), literary criticism (*Witches and Jesuits: Shakespeare's Macbeth*), and religion (*Why I Am a Catholic*). His most important works have dealt with American history. These include *Inventing America: Jefferson's Declaration of Independence; Nixon Agonistes: The Crisis of the Self-Made Man;* and *Explaining America: The Federalist*.

Wills won the 1992 Pulitzer Prize for *Lincoln at Gettysburg: The Words That Remade America*, a daring reinterpretation of Lincoln's Gettysburg Address. Wills argues that the speech that Lincoln delivered on November 19, 1863, for the dedication of the national cemetery at Gettysburg was the true turning point of the Civil War—more important than the battle fought there on July 1–3. The Union victory at Gettysburg was so grim and costly that it scarcely seemed a victory at all. But Lincoln's 272-word speech sanctified the battlefield, its fallen soldiers, and the war. It redefined the war as a struggle for human equality. According to Wills, the Gettysburg Address actually transformed America itself. In the following viewpoint, Wills relates how Lincoln seized his opportunity to turn the tide of history.

Not all the gallantry of [Confederate] General [Robert E.] Lee can redeem, quite, his foolhardiness at Gettysburg. When in doubt, he charged into the cannon's mouth—by proxy. Ordered afterward to assemble the remains of that doomed assault, [Confederate major general] George Pickett told Lee that he *had* no force to reassemble. Lee offered Jefferson Davis his resignation.

Nor did [Union] General [George] Meade, Lee's opposite number, leave Gettysburg in glory. Though he lost as many troops as Lee, he still had men and ammunition to pursue a foe who was running, at the moment, out of both. For a week, while Lincoln urged him on in an agony of obliterative hope, Meade let the desperate Lee lie trapped by a flooded Potomac. When, at last, Lee ghosted himself over the river, Lincoln feared the North would not persevere with the war through the next year's election. Meade, too, offered his resignation.

A Pattern of Pretense

Neither general's commander-in-chief could afford to accept these offers. Jefferson Davis had little but Lee's magic to rely on for repairing the effects of Lee's folly. (Romantic Southern fools cheered Lee wherever he rode on the day after his human sacrifice at Gettysburg.) Lincoln, on the other side, could not even vent his feelings by sending Meade the anguished letter he wrote him. A reprimand would ravel out the North's morale in long trains of recrimination. Both sides, leaving fifty thousand dead or wounded or missing behind them, had reason to maintain a large pattern of pretense about this battle—Lee pretending that he was not taking back to the South a broken cause, Meade that he had not let the broken pieces fall through his fingers. It would have been hard to predict that Gettysburg, out of all this muddle, these missed chances, all the senseless deaths, would become a symbol of national purpose, pride, and ideals. Abraham Lincoln transformed the ugly reality into something rich and strange—and he did it with 272 words. The power of words has rarely been given a more compelling demonstration.

The Debris of War

The residents of Gettysburg had little reason to feel satisfaction with the war machine that had churned up their lives. General Meade may have pursued Lee in slow motion; but he wired headquarters that "I cannot delay to pick up the debris of the battlefield." That debris was mainly a matter of rotting horseflesh and manflesh—thousands of fermenting bodies, with gas-distended bellies, deliquescing in the July heat. For hygienic reasons, the five thousand horses (or mules) had to be consumed by fire, trading the smell of burning flesh for that of decaying flesh. Eight thousand human bodies were scattered over, or (barely) under, the ground. Suffocating teams of soldiers, Confederate prisoners, and dragooned civilians slid the bodies beneath a minimal covering, as fast as possible—crudely posting the names of the Union dead with sketchy information on boards, not stopping to figure out what units the Confederate bodies had belonged to. It was work to be done hugger-mugger or not at all, fighting clustered bluebottle flies black on the earth, shoveling and retching by turns. The buzzards themselves had not stayed to share in this labor— days of incessant shelling had scattered them far off.

Even after most bodies were lightly blanketed, the scene was repellent. A nurse shuddered at the all-too-visible "rise and swell of human bodies" in these furrows war had plowed. A soldier noticed how earth "gave" as he walked over the shallow trenches. Householders had to plant around the bodies in their fields and gardens, or brace themselves to move the rotting corpses to another place. Soon these uneasy graves were being rifled by relatives looking for their dead—reburying other bodies they turned up, even more hastily (and less adequately) than had the first disposal crews. Three weeks after the battle, a prosperous Gettysburg banker, David Wills, reported to Pennsylvania's Governor [Andrew] Curtin: "In many instances arms and legs and sometimes heads protrude and my attention has been directed to several places where the hogs were actually rooting out the bodies and devouring them." . . .

The Need for Words

Curtin made the thirty-two-year-old David Wills his agent on the scene. Wills had studied law with Gettysburg's most prominent former citizen, Thaddeus Stevens, the radical Republican now representing Lancaster in Congress. Wills was a civic leader, and he owned the largest house on the town square. . . .

Wills . . . felt the need for artful words to sweeten the poisoned air of Gettysburg. He asked the principal wordsmiths of his time to join this effort—Longfellow, Whittier, Bryant. All three poets, each for his own reason, found their muse unbiddable. But Wills was not terribly disappointed. The normal purgative for such occasions was a large-scale solemn act of oratory, a kind of performance art with great power over audiences in the middle of the nineteenth century. Some later accounts would emphasize the length of the main speech at the Gettysburg dedication, as if that were an ordeal or an imposition on the audience. But a talk of several hours was customary and expected then—much like the length and pacing of a modern rock concert. The crowds that heard Lincoln debate Stephen Douglas in 1858, through three-hour engagements, were delighted to hear Daniel Webster and other orators of the day recite carefully composed paragraphs that filled two hours at the least.

Speakers Invited

The champion at such declamatory occasions, after the death of Webster, was Webster's friend Edward Everett. Everett was that rare thing, a scholar and Ivy-League diplomat who could hold mass audiences in thrall. His voice, diction, and gestures were successfully dramatic, and he always performed his carefully written text, no matter how long, from memory. Everett was the inevitable

The Gettysburg Address

Lincoln's Gettysburg Address, printed below, was a mere 272 words, spoken on November 19, 1863, in a space of about three minutes. It made no specific mention of any soldiers, the issue of slavery and emancipation, or even the name of the battle site. And yet it helped transform the war and the nation's ideals.

Four score and seven years ago our fathers brought forth on this continent, a new nation, conceived in Liberty, and dedicated to the proposition that all men are created equal.

Now we are engaged in a great civil war, testing whether that nation, or any nation so conceived and so dedicated, can long endure. We are met on a great battle-field of that war. We have come to dedicate a portion of that field, as a final resting place for those who here gave their lives that that nation might live. It is altogether fitting and proper that we should do this.

But, in a larger sense, we can not dedicate—we can not consecrate—we can not hallow—this ground. The brave men, living and dead, who struggled here, have consecrated it, far above our poor power to add or detract. The world will little note, nor long remember what we say here, but it can never forget what they did here. It is for us the living, rather, to be dedicated here to the unfinished work which they who fought here have thus far so nobly advanced. It is rather for us to be here dedicated to the great task remaining before us—that from these honored dead we take increased devotion to that cause for which they gave the last full measure of devotion—that we are here highly resolve that these dead shall not have died in vain—that this nation, under God, shall have a new birth of freedom—and that government of the people, by the people, for the people, shall not perish from the earth.

Abraham Lincoln, Gettysburg Address, November 19, 1863.

choice for Wills, the indispensable component in his scheme for the cemetery's consecration. Battlefields were something of a specialty with Everett—he had augmented the fame of Lexington and Concord and Bunker Hill by his oratory at those revolutionary sites. Simply to have him speak at Gettysburg would add this field to the sacred roll of names from the founder's battles. . . .

Lincoln must have been informally asked to attend, through his friend and bodyguard, Ward Lamon, by October 30, when he told a correspondent he meant to be present. . . . Though specifically invited to deliver only "a few appropriate remarks" to open the cemetery, he meant to use this opportunity. The partly mythical victory of Gettysburg was important to his administration's war propaganda. (There were, even now, few enough victories to boast of.) . . .

A Casual Composition

Lincoln seems—in familiar accounts—rather cavalier about preparing what he would say in Gettysburg. The silly but persistent myth is that he jotted his brief remarks on the back of an envelope. Better-attested accounts have him considering it on the way to a photographer's shop in Washington, writing it on a piece of cardboard as the train took him on the eighty-mile trip, penciling it in David Wills's house on the night before the dedication, writing it in that house on the morning of the day he had to deliver it, or even composing it in his head as Everett spoke, before Lincoln rose to follow him. . . .

These mythical accounts are badly out of character for Lincoln, who composed his speeches thoughtfully. His law partner, William Herndon, observing Lincoln's careful preparation of cases, records that he was a slow writer, who liked to sort out his points and tighten his logic and his phrasing. That is the process vouched for in every other case of Lincoln's memorable public statements. It is impossible to imagine him leaving his speech at Gettysburg to the last moment. He knew he would be busy on the train and at the site—important political guests were with him from his departure, and more joined him at Baltimore, full of talk about the war, elections, and policy. In Gettysburg he would be entertained at David Wills's house, with Everett and other important guests. State delegations would want a word with him. He hoped for a quick tour of the battle site (a hope fulfilled early on the nineteenth [of November 1863]). He could not count on any time for the concentration he required when weighing his words. . . .

Lincoln Prepares

A . . . reliable indication of Lincoln's preparation in Washington is provided by his consultation with the cemetery's landscaper. The President knew (presumably from talks with Lamon) that William Saunders of the Agriculture Department had conceived the grounds' plan and he called Saunders to the White House:

> A few days before the dedication of the grounds, President Lincoln sent word to me that he desired me to call at his office on the evening of the 17th [Tuesday], and take with me the plan of the cemetery. I was on hand at the appointed time, and spread the plan on his office table. He took much interest in it, asked about its surroundings, about Culp's Hill, Round Top, etc., and seemed familiar with the topography of the place although he had never been there. He was pleased with the method of the graves, said it differed from the ordinary cemetery, and, after I had explained the reasons, said it was an advisable and benefiting arrangement.

Lincoln no doubt retained some knowledge of the battle places from following reports during and after the three days of fighting there. Lamon, too, may have sketched the general scene as part of his "advancing" preparations over several weeks. But Lincoln's desire to have specific knowledge of the cemetery's features proves that he was not relying solely on a lightning stroke of genius to tell him what to say when he arrived on the spot.

Saunders's pride in his plan may color his reporting of Lincoln's reaction to it. But it is not unlikely that Lincoln approved of the careful way the graves were arranged so that (in Saunders's words) "the position of each [state] lot, and indeed of each interment, is relatively of equal importance." Lincoln would soon claim that these men died to vindicate "the proposition that all men are created equal." He would not, in his own speech, name a single individual, or distinguish officers from enlisted men (as Everett did in his tribute). In all this, his speech and Saunders's artifact are in aesthetic harmony. Each expressed the values of the other.

Lincoln at Gettysburg

Lincoln's train arrived toward dusk in Gettysburg [on November 18, 1863]. There were still coffins stacked at the station for completing the reburials. Wills and Everett met him and escorted him the two blocks to the Wills home, where dinner was waiting, along with several dozen other distinguished guests. Lincoln's black servant, William Slade, took his luggage to the second-story room where he would stay that night. It looked out on the square and the courthouse. . . .

Early in the morning, Lincoln and [Secretary of State William] Seward took a carriage ride to the battle sites. By eleven, Ward Lamon and his specially uninformed marshals were assigning horses to the various dignitaries (carriages would have clogged the site too much). The march was less than a mile, but Lamon had brought thirty horses into town, to join the hundred Wills supplied, for honoring the officials present.

Lincoln sat his horse gracefully (to the surprise of some), and looked meditative during the long wait while marshals tried to coax into line important people more concerned with their dignity than the President was with his. Lincoln was still wearing a mourning band on his hat for his dead son. He also wore white gauntlets, which made his large hands on the reins dramatic by contrast with his otherwise black attire. . . .

The Ceremony Begins

Everett had gone out earlier, by carriage, to prepare himself in the special tent he asked for near the platform. At sixty-nine, he had kidney trouble and needed to relieve himself just before and after the three-hour ceremony. (He had put his problem so delicately that his hosts did not realize that he meant to be left alone in the tent; but he finally coaxed them out.) Everett mounted the platform at the last moment after most of the others had arrived.

Those on the raised platform were hemmed close in by standing crowds. When it became clear that the numbers might approach twenty thousand, the platform was set at some distance from the burial operations. Only a third of the expected bodies had been buried, and those under fresh mounds. Other graves were readied for the bodies that arrived in irregular order (some from this state, some from that), making it impossible to complete one section at a time. The whole burial site was incomplete. Marshals tried to keep the milling thousands out of the work in progress.

Everett, as usual, had neatly placed his thick text on a little table before him—and then ostentatiously refused to look at it. He was able to indicate with gestures the sites of the battle's progress visible from where he stood. He excoriated the rebels for their atrocities, implicitly justifying the fact that some Confederate skeletons were still unburied, lying in the clefts of Devil's Den under rocks and autumn leaves. Two days earlier, Everett had been shown around the held, and places were pointed out where the bodies lay. His speech, for good or ill, would pick its way through the carnage. . . .

Three Minutes

When Lincoln rose, it was with a sheet or two, from which he read—as had the minister who offered the invocation. Lincoln's three minutes would, ever after, be obsessively contrasted with Everett's two hours in accounts of this day. It is even claimed that Lincoln disconcerted the crowd with his abrupt performance, so that people did not know how to respond ("Was that *all?*"). . . .

[But] there was only one "oration" announced or desired here. Though we call Lincoln's text *the* Gettysburg Address, that title clearly belongs to Everett. Lincoln's contribution, labeled "remarks," was intended to make the dedication formal (somewhat like ribbon-cutting at modern "openings"). . . .

A contrast of length with Everett's talk raises a false issue. Lincoln's text *is* startlingly brief for what it accomplished, but that would be equally true if Everett had spoken for a shorter time or had not spoken at all.

Lincoln's Performance

The contrast in other ways was strong. Everett's voice was sweet and expertly modulated; Lincoln's was high to the point of shrillness, and his Kentucky accent offended some Eastern sensibilities. But Lincoln derived an advantage from his high tenor voice—carrying power. If there is agreement on any one aspect of Lincoln's delivery, at Gettysburg and elsewhere, it is his audibility. Modern impersonators of Lincoln, like Walter Huston, Raymond Massey, Henry Fonda, and the various actors who give voice to Disneyland animations of the President, bring him before us as a baritone, which is considered a more manly or heroic voice—though both the Roosevelt presidents of [the twentieth] century were tenors. What should not be forgotten is that Lincoln was himself an actor, an expert raconteur and mimic, and one who spent hours reading speeches out of Shakespeare to any willing (and some unwilling) audiences. He knew a good deal about rhythmic delivery and meaningful inflections. John Hay, who had submitted to many of those Shakespeare readings, gave high marks to his boss's performance at Gettysburg. He put in his diary at the time that "the President, in a fine, free way, with more grace than is his wont, said his half dozen words of consecration." Lincoln's text was polished, his delivery emphatic, he was interrupted by applause five times. Read in a slow, clear way to the farthest listeners, the speech would take about three minutes. It is quite true that the audience did not take in all that happened in that short time— we are still trying to weigh the consequences of that amazing performance. But the myth that Lincoln was disappointed in the result—that he told the unreliable Lamon that his speech, like a bad plow, "won't scour"—has no basis. He had done what he wanted to do, and Hay shared the pride his superior took in an important occasion put to good use.

Lincoln's Achievement

At the least, Lincoln had far surpassed David Wills's hope for words to disinfect the air of Gettysburg. The tragedy of macerated bodies, the many bloody and ignoble aspects of this inconclusive encounter, are transfigured in Lincoln's rhetoric, where the physical residue of battle is volatilized as the product of an experiment *testing* whether a government can maintain the *proposition* of equality. The stakes of the three days' butchery are made intellectual, with abstract truths being vindicated. Despite verbal gestures to "that" battle and the men who died "here," there are no particulars mentioned by Lincoln—no names of men or sites or units, or even of sides (the Southerners are part of the "experiment," not foes mentioned in anger or rebuke). Everett succeeded with his audience by being thoroughly immersed in the details of the event he was celebrating. Lincoln eschews all local emphasis. His speech hovers far above the carnage. He lifts the battle to a level of abstraction that purges it of grosser matter—even "earth" is mentioned as the thing from which the tested form of government shall not perish. . . . Lincoln has aligned the dead in ranks of an ideal order. The nightmare realities have been etherealized in the crucible of his language.

But that was just the beginning of this complex transformation. Lincoln did for the whole Civil War what he accomplished for the single battlefield. He has prescinded from messy squabbles over constitutionality, sectionalism, property, states. Slavery is not mentioned, any more than Gettysburg is. The discussion is driven back and back, beyond the historical particulars, to great ideals that are made to grapple naked in an airy battle of the mind. Lincoln derives a new, a transcendental, significance from this bloody episode. Both North and South strove to win the battle for *interpreting* Gettysburg as soon as the physical battle had ended. Lincoln is after even larger game—he means to "win" the whole Civil War in ideological terms as well as military ones. And he will succeed: the Civil War *is*, to most Americans, what Lincoln wanted it to *mean*. Words had to complete the work of the guns.

A New Past, a New Future

Lincoln is here not only to sweeten the air of Gettysburg, but to clear the infected atmosphere of American history itself, tainted with official sins and inherited guilt. He would cleanse the Constitution—not, as William Lloyd Garrison had, by burning an instrument that countenanced slavery. He altered the document from within, by appeal from its letter to the spirit, subtly changing the recalcitrant stuff of that legal compromise, bringing it to its own indictment. By implicitly doing this, he performed one of the most daring acts of open-air sleight-of-hand ever witnessed by the unsuspecting. Everyone in that vast throng of thousands was having his or her intellectual pocket picked. The crowd departed with a new thing in its ideological luggage, that new constitution Lincoln had substituted for the one they brought there with them. They walked off, from those curving graves on the hillside, under a changed sky, into a different America. Lincoln had revolutionized the Revolution, giving people a new past to live with that would change their future indefinitely.

CHAPTER 4

What Is the Legacy of the Civil War?

✺ Chapter Preface

The late naturalist Stephen Jay Gould proposed a fascinating thought experiment. Rewind the "tape" of time back to a particular moment in history, erasing it as you go. Then record again from that moment and see what happens. Gould believed that history would never play out the same way twice. Chance and accident are too pervasive for historical events to unfold in a steady, predictable way.

Gould was writing about natural history, but his thought experiment applies equally well to human history. For instance, imagine rewinding the tape of time back to Lincoln's election in November 1860. Southern states would certainly secede—that much seems inevitable. But also imagine that Lincoln—perhaps counseled by different advisers—quietly withdrew the remaining federal troops from the seceding states. There would have been no firing on Fort Sumter, and perhaps no Civil War. As to how American history would have unfolded from that time on, opinions will surely differ.

Some historians are likely to argue that America would be better off today had there been no war. Perhaps the Union could have been restored by peaceful, diplomatic means. Perhaps emancipation could have been achieved (as it was in other parts of the world) gradually and peacefully, with slave owners financially compensated for their loss. Perhaps the United States would be more democratic today without the powerful federal government the war helped create.

Other historians would argue that the Civil War was an awful necessity. Without it, the Union might have continued to fragment, and so might the Confederacy. There would be no United States, only a conglomeration of independent territories, too quarrelsome and warlike for democracy to thrive in any of them. And since Southern slave owners had never showed any serious interest in emancipation, there seems no reason to assume that a peaceful, gradual end to slavery would have been feasible. The possibility that slavery might have continued down to the present day is certainly disturbing.

Of course, the Civil War *did* happen—and it was the most deadly and destructive war yet fought in human history. About 110,000 Union troops and about 94,000 Confederate troops died in battle. Many, many more died of disease caused largely by primitive and unsanitary medical conditions. Overall, the Union lost some 360,000 men, and the Confederacy some 258,000. The financial cost to the reunited nation has been estimated at about $20 billion.

But as the above thought experiment suggests, the war's legacy cannot be neatly assessed in facts and figures. The Union was restored, but never fully healed. Slavery was ended by the Thirteenth Amendment, but racial equality remains a troubling issue today. And if, as some historians suggest, the Civil War was the first true modern war, it opened the way for two world wars during the most violent century in human history. Such themes are explored in the following final viewpoints.

Viewpoint 1

"Modern war began to take shape here in America in the 1860's: and the agonizing uncertainty under which all of us have to live today is, I suppose, a part of our atonement."

The Civil War Was the First Modern War

Bruce Catton

The American historian Bruce Catton probably did more than any other author to give the reading public a realistic picture of the Civil War. With such books as *Mr. Lincoln's Army, Glory Road, The Coming Fury, Terrible Swift Sword*, and *Never Call Retreat*, Catton gained a reputation for vivid writing that more resembled immediate news reporting than history. In 1954 he won both the Pulitzer Prize and the National Book Award for *A Stillness at Appomattox.*

Catton's life gave him a unique perspective on the evolution of warfare during the nineteenth and twentieth centuries. As a child, he heard the reminiscences of elderly Civil War veterans. He served in the U.S. Navy during World War I and as a member of the U.S. War Production Board during World War II. Experience and research convinced him that the Civil War was the world's first truly modern war.

In the following viewpoint, taken from a 1958 lecture, Catton argues that the Civil War was modern not only in its weaponry,

Bruce Catton, *America Goes to War: The Civil War and Its Meaning in American Culture.* Hanover, NH: University Press of New England, 1958. Copyright © 1958 by William B. Catton. Reproduced by permission.

but in the deadly, unrestrained attitude of its combatants. More intriguingly, he proposes that the Civil War's very modernity was a central reason for its transformation into a war against slavery.

The Civil War was the first of the world's really modern wars. That is what gives it its terrible significance. For the great fact about modern war, greater even than its frightful destructiveness and its calculated, carefully applied inhumanity, is that it never goes quite where the men who start it intend that it shall go. Men do not control modern war; it controls them. It destroys the old bases on which society stood; and because it does, it compels men to go on and find the material for new bases, whether they want to do so or not. It has become so all-encompassing and demanding that the mere act of fighting it changes the conditions under which men live. Of all the incalculables which men introduce into their history, modern warfare is the greatest. If it says nothing else it says this, to all men involved in it, at the moment of its beginning: Nothing is ever going to be the same again.

Changes in Weaponry

The Civil War was the first modern war in two ways, and the first of these ways has to do with the purely technical aspect of the manner in which men go out to kill one another. That is to say that it was a modern war in the weapons that were used and in the way in which these affected the fighting.

On the surface, Civil War weapons look very old-fashioned; actually, they foreshadowed today's battles, and there are important parts of the Civil War which bear much more resemblance to World War I than to the Napoleonic Wars or to the American Revolution. Modern techniques were just coming into play, and they completely changed the conditions under which war would be waged.

Consider the weapons the Civil War soldiers used.

The infantryman's weapon was still spoken of as a musket—meaning a muzzle-loading smoothbore—and yet, by the time the war was a year or more old, nearly all infantrymen in that war carried rifles. These, to be sure, were still muzzle-loaders, but they were very different from the "Brown Bess" of tradition, the weapon on which all tactics and combat formations were still based.

With the old smoothbore, effective range—that is, the range at which massed infantry fire would hit often enough to be adequately damaging—was figured at just about one hundred yards. I believe it was U.S. Grant himself who remarked that with the old musket a man might shoot at you all day, from a distance of one hundred and fifty yards or more, without even making you aware that he was doing it.

Old Tactics

The point of infantry tactics in 1861 is that they depended on this extreme limitation of the infantry's effective field of fire. A column of assault, preparing to attack an enemy position, could be massed and brought forward with complete confidence that until it got to comparatively close range nothing very damaging could happen to it. From that moment on, everything was up to the determination and numbers of the attackers. Once they had begun to charge, the opposing line could not possibly get off more than one or two shots per man. If the assaulting column had a proper numerical advantage, plus enough discipline and leadership to keep it moving forward despite losses, it was very likely to succeed.

The assaulting column always went in with fixed bayonets, because any charge that was really driven home would wind up with hand-to-hand fighting. And if the assailants could get to close quarters with a fair advantage in numbers, either the actual use of the bayonet or the terrible threat of it would finish the business.

Artillery, properly massed, might change the picture. The smoothbore field pieces of the old days were indeed of limited range, but they very greatly out-ranged the infantry musket, and if a general had enough guns banked up at a proper spot in his defensive line he could count on breaking up a charging column, or at least on cutting it open and destroying its cohesion, before it got within infantry range. The antidote to this, on the part of the offense, was often the cavalry charge: massed cavalry squadrons could come in to sabre the gunners . . . and make the defensive line something that could be left to the foot soldier and his bayonet.

Up to 1861, all the intricate bits of infantry drill which the re-cruits had to learn, and all of the professional thinking of the generals who directed their movements, were based on weapons of limited range and tactics of rather personal assault.

Then, suddenly, the whole business went out of date, just because weapons had changed.

The rifled Springfield or Enfield was a very different arm from the old smoothbore. It looked about the same, it was still a muzzle-loader, and today it looks just as much like a museum piece. But it had ever so much more range and accuracy, and it completely changed the way in which men fought.

Deadly Marksman

With the Civil War rifle a good marksman could hit and kill an opponent at somewhere between half a mile and a mile. The weapon's effective range, of course, was a good deal less than that, but an infantry line could still inflict destructive fire on its opponents at two or three times the distance that was possible with the old smoothbore. A decisive engagement could, and often did, take place with the opposing lines more than a quarter of a mile apart. At Antietam, according to an account written after the war, a veteran in the Army of the Potomac said that his unit and a Confederate unit got into action at close quarters; and this, he wrote reflectively, was one of the few battles in all the war in which he actually saw his enemies. Most of the time, "the enemy" was simply a line of snake-rail fence or a grove of trees or a raw length of heaped-up earth, from which came clouds of powder smoke and a storm of bullets. To see the other fellow as a recognizable human being was actually rather unusual—so much so that this veteran noted the fact, when it did happen, in his postwar reminiscences.

All of this meant that the old manner of making an attack was no longer good. To mass an assaulting column and drive it in with the men moving elbow to elbow was simply to invite destruction. It did work now and then, to be sure, if there were especial circumstances to aid the offensive, but under ordinary circumstances it did not work at all. . . .

Artillery and Cavalry

Things changed for the artillery and cavalry, too. By the middle of the Civil War, artillery that was massed in a defensive line along with the infantry was subjected to killing fire by sharpshooters. Its old advantage was pared down sharply. Many striking things were indeed done by brave gunners who moved their pieces into the front line, and soldiers like John Pelham and Hubert Dilger showed an amazing ability to use their guns at close range; but, in the main, artillery suffered intensely from the infantry's increased range of fire, and the artillerist dreaded infantry fire a good deal more than he dreaded counter-battery fire.

Things were even worse for the cavalry. It became nothing short of suicide for cavalry to attack formed infantry, or artillery with infantry support, and it was rarely even tried. Cavalry became less and less a combat arm, in major battles, although of course it remained extremely important because of its use as a scouting arm and as a means of screening an army's movements.

Slowness to Change

It took the generals a long time to adjust themselves to the change which had occurred while the war was going on. Many things about Civil War battles which are otherwise inexplicable become clear enough when the sudden modernization in weapons is taken into account. The repeated, disastrous frontal assaults, the frightful toll of casualties, the fact that a hard battle often left the victor too mangled to make an effective pursuit, the final turn to trench warfare—all of these things simply reflect the fact that the weapons which the soldier used in the Civil War had completely changed the conditions under which he could use them. Many of the tragedies and apparent blunders in that war came simply because the generals were trained to tactics which were worse than useless. For all of its muzzle-loaders, its dashing cavalry actions, and its archaic artillery, the Civil War was nevertheless a modern war.

A Ruthless Mentality

But it was more than just a matter of weapons. Much more important is the fact that the mental attitude of the two governments involved—which of course is to say the mental attitudes of the opposing peoples themselves—had that peculiar, costly, ruthless cast which is the great distinguishing mark of modern warfare.

Neither side in the Civil War was prepared to stop anywhere short of complete victory. In the old days, wars had been formalized; two nations fought until it seemed to one side or the other that it would not be worth while to fight any longer, and then some sort of accommodation would be reached—and, in the last analysis, nothing would have been changed very much. But in the Civil War it was all or nothing. The Southern States wanted absolute independence, and the Northern States wanted absolute union; once a little blood had been shed, there was no half-way point at which the two sides could get together and make a compromise. So the stakes were immeasurably increased, and this too affected the way in which men fought. If you are fighting a total war, the enemy's army is not your sole target. What you are really shooting at is his ability to carry on the fight, which means you will hit him wherever you can with any weapon that comes to your hand.

Anything Goes

Probably it is this more than any other single thing that is the distinguishing mark of modern war: anything goes. The old "rules of civilized warfare" which loom so large in the textbooks simply disappear. Making war becomes a matter of absolutes; you cannot stop anywhere short of complete victory. Your enemy's army remains one of your targets, to be sure, but if you can destroy the social and economic mechanism which supports that army, and thereby can cause the army itself to collapse, you have gone a long way toward reaching your goal.

Consider for a moment the logical implications of this attitude. Ultimately, it is nothing less than the road to horror. It obliterates the moralities and the restraints which the race has so carefully built up through many generations. If it has any kind of rational base, the rationale is nothing much loftier than a belief that the end justifies the means. It can—and does—put an entire nation at the mercy of its most destructive instincts. What you do to your enemy comes, at last, to be limited not by any reluctance to inflict pain, misery, and death, and not by any feeling that there are limits to the things which a civilized people may do, but solely by your technical capacity to do harm. Without suffering any pangs of conscience, the group becomes prepared to do things which no single member of the group would for a moment contemplate.

By present-day standards, this process was not carried very far in our Civil War, but the genesis was there. The thing that makes modern war so appallingly frightful is not so much the hideous things which in our sublime innocence we call "weapons" as it is the development of an attitude which makes the unlimited use of those weapons something that is taken for granted. This attitude affected not only the way in which the Civil War itself was fought but the results that came out of the war.

Destructiveness Pays

This dawning notion of all-out war changed the way in which the Union soldier, for example, fought. He quickly came to see that anything which hurt the Confederacy's ability to carry on the war brought Northern victory just that much nearer. It "paid," for instance, to tear up railway lines in the South, to destroy iron foundries and textile mills and machine shops, to cut off the sources of raw material which enabled the Confederacy to maintain the fight. It very soon became apparent that it was necessary—using that word in its military context—to cripple the South's ability to feed its civilians and its armies. The farmer's property, in other words, was a military objective; to destroy barns and corn cribs, to drive off herds of cattle and hogs, to kill horses and mules—these acts became definite matters of military desirability. If a state or a section whose pork and corn and cotton enabled the Confederacy to fight were reduced to destitution, the Confederacy was that much weaker and hence that much nearer final destruction.

So we got, in that war, immense destructive raids which had much the same justification that the air raid has today. From sending a [Union general William] Sherman through Georgia, with the avowed objective of destroying that state's productive capacity, or from sending a [calvary leader Philip] Sheridan down the Shenandoah Valley under instructions to reduce that rich granary to a condition under which a crow flying across it would have

The heavy artillery and unrestrained violence of the Northern troops left cities like Charleston, South Carolina, in ruins at the end of the war.

to carry his own rations—from doing that to dispatching a flight of bombing planes to reduce a manufacturing city to smoking rubble is only a step. Modern war began to take shape here in America in the 1860's: and the agonizing uncertainty under which all of us have to live today is, I suppose, a part of our atonement.

Changing Objectives

In any case, fighting that kind of war leads you to objectives you had not had when the fighting began. This is exactly what happened in the Civil War. The Union soldier, invading the South, had as one of his objectives the destruction of Southern property. The most obvious, easily-removed piece of property in all of Dixie was the Negro slave. Even the Northerner who believed in slavery came to see that, and he came to see it quickly. The mere fact that he thought the black man ought to be a slave led him to understand that this slave, this bit of strangely animate property, was an asset to the government that was trying to destroy the Union. Other kinds of property were to be destroyed. This particular kind could not exactly be destroyed—after all, it was somehow human—but it could be taken away from its owners and thereby rendered useless.

Dismantling Slavery

It took the Northern armies only a very short time to learn this lesson. As soon as they had learned it, they began to take the institution of chattel slavery apart, chattel by chattel, not because they had anything against it but because they wanted to win the war.

Bear in mind, now, that most of this work was done by men who had no intention whatever, when they enlisted, of making war to end slavery. Slavery was killed by the act of war itself. It was the one human institution on all the earth which could not possibly be defended by force of arms, because that force, once called into play, was bound to destroy it. The Union armies which ended slavery were led by men like [Union general Ulysses S.] Grant and Sherman, who had profound sympathies with the South and who had never in their lives shown the slightest sympathies with the abolitionists. But they were also men who believed in the one great, fearful fact about modern war—that when you get into it, the guiding rule is that you have to win it. They made hard war, in other words, and hard war in the 1860's meant the end of human slavery.

So Grant and Sherman led armies down through Tennessee into the deep South, striking hard as they went. They struck slavery simply because it was in the way; striking it, they gave it its death blow.

Black Allies

It is interesting to note that along with all of this the Northern soldiers who destroyed slavery came, almost in spite of themselves, to see that the slaves whom they were liberating had claims on their own humanity. The Federal soldier who went South was moving into a hostile land, where he could count on having the enmity of everyone he encountered. Yet in all of this he quickly discovered that he had allies—black folk, who had only the vaguest understanding of what the war was all about but who did somehow see that these heavy-handed young men in blue uniforms were on their side . . . or, if not exactly on their side, at least against their masters, against the system which held them in subjection and numbered them with the ox and the mule as animate chattels. The Federal who wanted to know where Southern armies were and what they were doing had only to ask the nearest Negro; to the best of his knowledge—which usually was pretty limited—the Negro would faithfully tell him. The Federal who had got separated from his command and wanted to find his way back would go to the slave as an ally, and the slave would help him. The Northern boy who had managed to escape from a Southern prison and who, from the bottom of Georgia or South Carolina, sought to tramp the weary miles back to a Federal army camp, knew that the first Negro cabin he came to would be a haven of refuge, a place where he might get something to eat, concealment, a chance to rest, and guidance on his perilous way.

Seeing all of this, the Northern soldier at last came to see that these black folk who were somehow on his side were not just stray bits of property; they were people, people who would do him a good turn if they possibly could, friends on whom he could call in the deepest pit of danger or hardship.

War for Union and Freedom

When the Northern government began to fight the Civil War it explicitly disavowed any intention of making war on slavery. By Presidential pronouncement and by specific act of Congress it stated that it was fighting to restore the Union and to do no more than that; the "domestic institutions" of the individual states—meaning slavery—were not involved at all. Yet the mere act of fighting the war killed that program in little more than one year. By the beginning of 1863 the Northern government had proclaimed the emancipation of slaves. The war now was being fought for union *and* for freedom—a most substantial broadening of its base. And this change had come about, not especially because anyone had done a lot of hard, serious thinking about the evils of slavery, but primarily because the change had to come if the war was to be won. The war itself had enforced the change. It had done so because it was, in the strictest sense, a modern war—a war of unlimited objectives and of unpredictable results.

Viewpoint 2

"Rather than being the first of the 'modern' wars, the Civil War was the last conflict of the Napoleonic era."

The Civil War Was Not a Modern War

Stuart L. Koehl

Throughout the countless historical debates and controversies surrounding the Civil War, there long seemed to be one point of agreement and certainty: The Civil War was the first truly modern war—or at the very least, a transitional war that paved the way for the terrible wars of the twentieth century. But even this piece of conventional wisdom fell into doubt during the 1980s with the publication of British military historian Paddy Griffith's meticulously researched book *Battle Tactics of the Civil War.*

Griffith argued that the Civil War was not a modern war at all—that it actually resembled the wars fought by Napoleon Bonaparte around the turn of the nineteenth century. According to Griffith, the modernity of the Civil War is a myth fostered by such factors as Americans' chauvinistic desire to be first at everything and historians' wrongheaded fascination with technological gadgetry.

In the following viewpoint, Stuart L. Koehl—himself a military historian and the coauthor of *A Dictionary of Modern War*—concisely summarizes Griffith's ideas and research.

Stuart L. Koehl, "'Modern' Civil War Was Really Napoleonic," *The Washington Times*, February 3, 1996. Copyright © 1996 by News World Communications, Inc. Reproduced by permission.

With the introduction of rifled firearms, use of railroads, steamships, telegraph, the dominance of the tactical defensive, and the indecisive outcome of most battles, the Civil War is said to presage the industrial mode of warfare epitomized by World War I.

The historical evidence, however, offers an alternative interpretation: Rather than being the first of the "modern" wars, the Civil War was the last conflict of the Napoleonic era.

On the operational and tactical level, technological developments had little impact during the Civil War: Armies still went into battle on foot or on horseback, orders were still transmitted verbally or in writing by the commander or aides on horses; a general had little control over forces outside his own field of view—exactly the conditions faced by generals for the preceding 200 years.

Offense and Defense

On the battlefield itself, it is usually asserted that the introduction of the rifled musket, firing the conical Minie ball, greatly increased the range and accuracy of infantry firepower. It upset the balance between offense and defense, reduced the utility of artillery and cavalry, and in general made attack more difficult, if not impossible. Thus battles became both more costly and less decisive than in previous wars.

This interpretation has two major flaws. First, it ignores battlefield trends dating back more than a century before the Civil War; second, it considers only the technical dimension of war and ignores the critical "soft factors."

From the Seven Years War (1755–1763), it had become increasingly obvious that the tactical defensive was stronger than the offensive. As artillery increased in both quantity and technical effectiveness, successful attacks became rarer and more expensive. In both the number and percentage of casualties, many European battles (Zorndorf, 1757; Kunersdorf, 1758; Torgau, 1759; Wagram, 1809; Borodino, 1812; Leipzig, 1813; Waterloo, 1815) equalled or exceeded those of the Civil War.

Nor was decisive battle the norm in the preceding century: For every Austerlitz [Moravia, 1805] or Waterloo [Belgium, 1815], there were many more battles in which the loser withdrew battered but intact. Armies had simply become too large, too well-articulated (with organization into standing divisions and corps) and too easily reconstituted to overwhelm in a single battle.

The Rifled Musket

Doctrine, training, leadership and morale contribute far more to the outcome of battles than mere firepower. For example, take the case of the rifled musket.

In theory, it has a maximum effective range of more than 480 yards (vs. 120 yards for a smoothbore musket). Attacking infantry could cover that distance in about four minutes, during which time defending infantry would be able to fire about eight volleys. Assume that the attackers and defenders both have 500 men. If each volley scores only 20 percent hits, the attackers should suffer 344 casualties during the advance (though each volley should increase in lethality as the range closed).

If this is correct, attack would not only be impossible, but firefights could never last more than a few minutes.

But a cursory examination of real Civil War battles reveals numerous instances of firefights lasting more than an hour, without the devastating casualties that might be expected. Why?

Startling Statistics

In "Battle Tactics of the Civil War," British military historian Paddy Griffith attempts to answer this question through "tactical snippeting," micro-analyses of 113 specific engagements. By considering the time each unit spent in combat, the number of rounds it expended and the casualties it suffered (and inflicted), Mr. Griffith was able to compile statistics for typical engagement ranges and casualty rates in infantry firefights.

His results are startling: The typical Civil War firefight occurred not at 400 yards, but a mere 127—only a marginally greater range than in the smoothbore era.

Further, these firefights were singularly protracted. Thus, at Brawner Farm, during Second Manassas, the Union Iron Brigade and the Confederate Stonewall Division exchanged volleys from 6 to 9 P.M., at a range of 60 to 100 yards, during which time the Iron Brigade suffered a total of 751 casualties out of some 2,100 men engaged, or an average 4.71 casualties per minute—not exactly falling in windrows. Other hard-fought actions yield similar results.

Smoke and Fear

Throughout the war, attacking units were normally able to get well within Napoleonic ranges of the defending line, and could remain for considerable periods without suffering annihilation.

The most important factor accounting for the disparity between the theoretical and actual effectiveness of rifled musketry is suppression, or the psychological effects of firepower. The battlefield is not a target range, and a marksman able to hit the bull's-eye at several hundred yards may be unable to hit a man at only a few dozen because of the suppressive effect of noise, smoke and above all, fear.

Terrain is another factor: The real world is not a billiard table, and even small undulations can create enough "dead ground" to shelter troops from direct fire; lines of sight rarely extend more than 200 to 300 yards, dropping to only a few dozen in the close terrain.

Moreover, black powder propellant quickly cloaked the battlefield in dense gray smoke, reducing visibility to 100 yards or less, and making accurate fire difficult.

Perhaps even more important, few units actually were trained to deliver aimed fire. Target practice was rare, and when scheduled, tended to stress speed of fire, perhaps because officers recognized that smoke, terrain and suppression made long-range engagements unlikely.

Thus, while there were some units (like [Col. Hiram C.] Berdan's Sharpshooters) capable of long-range, aimed fire, most units were unable to hit anything beyond 100 to 200 yards.

The Mirror Image

If firepower was unable to prevent units from closing with each other, why were there relatively few instances of infantry carrying positions by assault?

Mr. Griffith finds compelling evidence in the training and doctrine employed by officers both North and South. It must be remembered that most of the senior officers on both sides were products of West Point, leading to a unique "mirror imaging" phenomenon. The antebellum West Point was above all an engineering school; the small, frontier Army had little need for tacticians, and a great need for men able to survey, draw maps, dredge rivers and build forts.

The approach to tactics advocated at West Point, therefore, reflected a peculiar "engineering" orientation based on firepower and field fortifications. Cadets were indoctrinated to believe that intrenchments could be taken (at great cost) only by long-term professional troops.

As the small size of the prewar Army dictated that any large-scale conflict would be fought mainly by short-term volunteers, officers developed tactical and operational concepts that emphasized firepower and positional defense. Few, if any, officers understood or advocated the use of "shock tactics" based on closing with the enemy and breaking his morale.

The Psychology

The sketchy training of the first volunteer regiments (and their junior officers), plus the results of the first Civil War battles, only reinforced this prejudice against shock action. Union Gen. William T. Sherman thus could ridicule the bayonet as good only for roasting potatoes.

While modern analysts point out that bayonets accounted for only 0.8 percent of all casualties, this misses the point: In shock action, one side or the other usually breaks before the attacker closes. As Gen. George S. Patton put it, "Battles are determined not by how many get killed, but by how many get scared."

While Civil War infantry usually could get to within 100 yards of the enemy line, significant psychological (rather than physical) impediments prevented pressing the assault home. Above all, this was a problem of leadership, morale and perceptions.

During the advance, the attacker took casualties, and the urge to respond was great. But once allowed to halt and return fire, it proved almost impossible to get men moving again.

Only strong, resolute leadership and high morale would allow a unit to advance, without stopping, into the enemy position. Few units—and fewer leaders—had those characteristics.

But how could the same units endure protracted and indecisive exposure for hours on the firing line? Part of the explanation lies in the expectations of the officers. They had little faith in the ability of their citizen-soldiers to storm rifle pits or trench lines, and were inclined to halt and shoot it out. This attitude tended to transfer itself to the troops, who also became shy of intrenchments.

All of these factors combined to favor fire over shock, which almost guaranteed that any battle would be prolonged, bloody and indecisive.

Artillery

Another shibboleth of the Civil War is that the rifled musket seriously reduced the effectiveness of artillery by rendering gun crews vulnerable to infantry fire.

But given the effective range of Civil War musketry, this could not be true; a survey of artillery units indicates that casualty rates were only a fraction of those in infantry units (and mostly caused by artillery fire).

Some argue that artillery was less effective than in previous wars. After all, only about 8 percent of casualties were inflicted by artillery. This may be misleading since it is based on observations of field surgeons, who examined only those not killed outright. So the best that can be said is that artillery caused only 8 percent of all wounds. But roundshot and canister [large pellets fired in clusters from cannon] were more likely to be instantly fatal than the smaller musket ball.

The lack of massed batteries in the Napoleonic style is stressed as further evidence that artillery had been eclipsed. But the heavily wooded and rolling terrain of the United States normally did not permit the massing of more than 12 to 18 guns. Where massed batteries could be assembled, they were—such as at Second Manassas, Antietam, Fredericksburg and Gettysburg.

Then, too, there were few officers on either side with sufficient experience or insight to use artillery *en masse:* Gen. Henry Hunt for the Union, and Cols. Stephen D. Lee and E. Porter Alexander for the Confederacy are among the exceptions. Some also have noted that artillery was seldom used "offensively"—i.e., pushed up to within 100 yards of the enemy, again, in a Napoleonic manner.

The perceived (if not the actual) lethality of artillery also exerted a psychological effect on an attacker. It disrupted formations, often breaking an attack without infantry assistance.

Almost all of Lee's assaults at Malvern Hill were shattered by artillery alone, as was Union Gen. Fitz John Porter's final attack on Stonewall Jackson at Second Manassas. Hunt, the Army of the Potomac's chief of artillery, believed that [Gen. George E.] Pickett's Charge could have been defeated by artillery alone, had more batteries been engaged.

Cavalry

The rifled musket also is supposed to have rendered cavalry useless in battle, relegating it to scouting and raiding. Several failed cavalry charges (e.g., Union Gen. Elon Farnsworth's attack at Gettysburg) are said to prove the point. But this statement, too, does not hold up to closer scrutiny.

Heavily wooded terrain made mass employment of cavalry problematic. In addition, it takes much longer to train cavalry than infantry, which made raising a large cavalry corps difficult. Finally, from an army that had only two cavalry regiments before 1860, it was even more difficult to find officers with the knowledge and experience to lead large bodies of horsemen.

Thus, from the beginning of the war, cavalry were frittered away. That, in turn, reinforced the biases of firepower-oriented infantry officers against a shock role for cavalry (similar views emerged about the tank before World War II).

This situation was not rectified until the end of 1863, when the revitalized Union cavalry under Alfred Pleasanton, and then Philip Sheridan, devised tactics combining both mounted and dismounted action based on firepower and shock.

Employed by aggressive brigade and division commanders such as George Custer and Wesley Merritt, these tactics allowed the Union cavalry to play major battlefield roles at Winchester, Cedar Creek, Saylor's Creek, Appomattox and Selma.

A Matter of Dogma

From this cursory examination it can be seen that there were few, if any, technological developments in the Civil War that fundamentally altered the Napoleonic battlefield equation (repeating firearms might have, but were numerically insignificant).

To the inability of commanders to understand and employ shock tactics must be added the failure of senior commanders to coordinate forces and employ combined arms tactics. This should not be surprising, considering the small size of the prewar Army. Most regular officers had never commanded anything larger than a company.

Handling large forces in battle requires practice backed up by competent staff work; both were in short supply at the start of the war, but successful commanders, North and South, demonstrated a steep learning curve.

By 1864, much of the bumbling that had characterized the early war was gone. But it was too late to overcome the prejudice against shock tactics imparted during the first years—it had become a matter of dogma from general to private. For all that, however, the tactics and the nature of the battlefield were still much closer to Waterloo in 1815, than Loos [France] in 1915.

The distinction of the first of the modern wars must go to the Franco-Prussian War (1870–71), which really did see the widespread use of breech-loading weapons, machine guns and steel, breech-loading cannon that made the old, Napoleonic tactics finally, and irrevocably, obsolete.

Viewpoint 3

"The South had thrown her life into the scales and lost it."

The Confederacy Was a Tragic Lost Cause

Woodrow Wilson

Woodrow Wilson, the twenty-eighth president of the United States, is best remembered for leading America during World War I and helping to found the League of Nations. It was he who first spoke of making "the world safe for democracy." But before turning to politics, Wilson was a scholar and historian. In 1902, he became the president of Princeton University; that same year, he completed the five volumes of *A History of the American People*, from which the following viewpoint has been adapted.

Wilson was born in Virginia in 1856. As a young boy, he witnessed the Civil War's ravaging effects on the South. Later, as a historian, he argued the moral rightness of the Northern cause and praised the restoration of the Union, but he remained at heart a Southerner and sympathized deeply with the Confederacy.

In the following viewpoint, Wilson argues that it was the South's tragedy to be lost in the past—a feudal society in an increasingly industrial world. Hugely overwhelmed by the manpower and military technology of the Union, the Confederacy was doomed to defeat from its very founding. There is a note of

Woodrow Wilson, *A History of the American People: Critical Changes and Civil War*. New York: Harper & Brothers, 1902.

187

nostalgia in Wilson's description of a South that perished for principle, as if a certain archaic nobility had been lost to the world.

The nation, shaken by those four never to be forgotten years of awful war, could not return to the thoughts or to the life that had gone before them. An old age had passed away, a new age had come in, with the sweep of that stupendous storm. Everything was touched with the change it had wrought. Nothing could be again as it had been. The national consciousness, disguised, uncertain, latent until that day of sudden rally and call to arms, had been cried wide awake by the voices of battle, and acted like a passion now in the conduct of affairs. All things took their hue and subtle transformation from it: the motives of politics, the whole theory of political action, the character of the government, the sentiment of duty, the very ethics of private conduct were altered as no half century of slow peace could have altered them.

Sacrifice and Loss

The sheer cost, the unspeakable sacrifices of the desperate struggle, made ineffaceable record of themselves in the thoughts and purposes of people and politicians alike. What had been spent to fight the fight out passed calculation. It had cost the country more than seven hundred men for every day of all the four long years of campaign and battle: four hundred killed or mortally wounded on the field, the rest dead of disease exposure, accident, or the slow pains of imprisonment. . . .

In the North four men out of every nine of the military population had been enlisted for a service of three years in the field: in all 1,700,000 out of a military population of 4,600,000. Of these three hundred and sixty thousand had lost their lives; one hundred and ten thousand by the actual casualties of the field. But the sacrifices of the South had been greater yet,—immeasurably greater. The North had spent out of its abundance; the South had spent all that it had, and was stripped naked of its resources. While the war lasted it had been stripped naked also of its men. Nine men out of every ten of fighting age had gone from country-sides and towns to the field, reckoning only those who enlisted for at least three out of the four years of the struggle. Before the war ended mere half grown boys and men grown old were included in the muster. The total military population of the South was but 1,065,000. Nine hundred thousand of these she drew into her armies for at least three years of service. The lives of close upon three hundred thousand she gave as her sacrifice of blood,—more than one-fourth of all fit for the field. Ninety-four thousand lost their lives in actual battle. South Carolina lost one-fourth of her military population by the casualties of the field. The armed hosts and power of the North increased as the strength and resources of the South diminished. . . .

The Southern Disaster

The southerners . . . , paroled at their surrender, and humanely bidden keep their horses for the spring ploughing, turned back to fields swept bare and desolate, villages whose life had first languished and then stood still, towns without trade or industry, where everything waited to be planned and begun anew, as if there had been no past to place foot upon. Their country had indeed, as General [Robert E.] Lee said, to be "built up on a new basis." They carried back to it no smallest part of what the ravages and untold costs of war had stripped away. Their lives were divested of everything that belonged to the age gone by save only their thoughts: thoughts of irreparable loss, of principles long revered but now discredited, of a social order cut up by the roots, of a life thrust away to be henceforth a mere bitter memory, of a future of new effort to be faced with all the pains of utter disaster thick upon them.

A World Lost in Time

Travellers from over sea had said that to cross the line between North and South was like passing from one century to another. In the one section they found an almost antique order of life, changed scarcely at all from that which settlers out of the elder England of the Stuarts [the British Royal Family 1603–1714] and the Prince of Orange [King William III] had established in Virginia and the Carolinas; in the other, all that belonged to the modern world,—communities quick with the movements of a various commerce, busy with mining, manufactures, the construction of railways, the diversification of industry. The South kept still the social order and the social and political ideals of an elder genera-tion. Slavery gave it a touch half mediæval, half oriental. There was something of the patriarchal way of life in the broad country-sides where masters of fields and flocks and herds went in and out upon their errands of superintendence among groups of dusky slaves; something, too, that recalled the mediæval lord and his serfs. And yet there was the air of the nineteenth century, too, the touch of democracy, in the plain and wholesome simplicity of the planters' lives, and their frank comradeship with all their neigh-bors who were of their own privilege of citizenship. The com-merce of the modern world passed in and out at the southern ports as at those of the North. Southern merchants felt the spirit of the times in all their enterprises; railways brought the products of every land and region to their shops and warehouses; the im-pulses of the world and of its changing thought stirred there as elsewhere. What held the South back in the way of the older cen-turies was its unaltered, its unalterable social order, which be-longed to the age in which the constitution had been devised, not to that in which its whole spirit and operation had been subtly changed by the pervasive processes of national growth. . . .

Losing Heart at Last

No one could wonder to see even a people such as the southern-ers had shown themselves to be lose heart at last, acknowledge the bitter fortunes of [the war's] last days intolerable, and yield in a sort of despair. It had taken all the vigor and audacity of their gov-ernment to keep them to the hopeless business as the year 1864 disclosed what it had in store for them. Not a little of the dogged perseverance and undaunted action of those closing months of the struggle had been due to the masterful characteristics of Mr. Jefferson Davis, the President of the Confederacy. He had served a distinguished apprenticeship in arms in the Mexican war [1846–1848], a still more distinguished apprenticeship in affairs in the cabinet and in the Senate of the United States. He had the pride, the spirit of initiative, the capacity in business which qualify men for leadership, and lacked nothing of indomitable will and imperious purpose to make his leadership effective. What he did lack was wisdom in dealing with men, willingness to take the judgment of others in critical matters of business, the instinct which recognizes ability in others and trusts it to the utmost to play its

The Perils of Emancipation

In his historical writings, Woodrow Wilson criticized slavery only mildly and even found positive things to say about it—for example, that it was an advancement for blacks over African civilization. In a 1901 article for the Atlantic Monthly, *Wilson reserved much harsher criticism for postwar emancipation, which he saw as disastrously mishandled.*

An extraordinary and very perilous state of affairs had been created in the South by the sudden and absolute emancipation of the negroes, and it was not strange that the southern legislatures should deem it necessary to take extraordinary steps to guard against the manifest and pressing dangers which it entailed. Here was a vast "laboring, landless, homeless class," once slaves, now free; unpracticed in liberty, unschooled in self-control; never sobered by the discipline of self-support, never established in any habit of prudence; excited by a freedom they did not understand, exalted by false hopes; bewildered and without leaders, and yet insolent and aggressive; sick of work, covetous of pleasure,—a host of dusky children untimely put out of school. In some of the states they outnumbered the whites,—notably in Mississippi and South Carolina. They were a danger to themselves as well as to those whom they had once served, and now feared and suspected; and the very legislatures which had accepted the Thirteenth Amendment hastened to pass laws which should put them under new restraints.

Woodrow Wilson, "The Reconstruction of the Southern States," *Atlantic Monthly*, January 1901.

independent part. He too much loved to rule, had too overween-ing a confidence in himself, and took leave to act as if he under-stood much better than those did who were in actual command what should be done in the field. He let prejudice and his own wil-ful judgment dictate to him the removal of [General] Joseph E. Johnston from the command at Atlanta, the only man who could have made [General William T.] Sherman's march to the sea im-possible. He sought to control too many things with too feminine a jealousy of any rivalry in authority. But his spirit was the life of the government. His too frequent mistakes were the result as much of the critical perplexities of an impossible task as of weak-ness of character. He moved direct, undaunted by any peril, and heartened a whole people to hold steadfast to the end.

Exhaustion and Despair

The end came with every sign of sheer exhaustion and despair. Many a southern man had gone into that terrible contest against his better judgment, not wishing to see the Union broken, but yielding to his neighbors' views and the challenge of the summons to arms. Such men were a minority, here and there very strong, but nowhere strong enough to make their will prevalent in affairs; and they had very loyally offered their lives and their property for the cause they would rather have seen vindicated in some other way. When those last days came they took heart to acknowledge the inevitable, and to urge peace as a mere means to avoid utter destruction. While they cried to their rulers peace seemed to come almost of itself. The southern armies melted away by wholesale desertion. There was nothing to eat, there was next to nothing to put into the guns themselves; the women and children at home were starving as well as the men in the camps, their only helpers and protectors. It was more than the human spirit could bear. Men turned by the hundreds, by the thousands, by the tens of thousands from the camps to the roads which led homeward. The end had manifestly come. There was no need to stay to see it come. If they stayed at all, how could they leave until it came; and how could the women and children wait? When the surrender came federal rations had to be served out to those who were left to save them from the helpless weakness of starvation.

And so their land was to be "built up on a new basis," as General Lee said. The South had thrown her life into the scales and lost it. There had been extraordinary devotion and heroism and mastery on both sides,—in the South a devotion and sacrifice hardly to be matched save in some war of religion; armies of the same race and breeding had met and neither had known how to yield; the end could not come until one or the other was overwhelmed; the South had been overwhelmed; and the most terrible war of modern times was over. Statesmen and patriots might well look about them and see with a sort of dismay what there was to be reconstructed throughout the whole fabric of the national life. The Union had been saved; it was yet to be rehabilitated.

Viewpoint 4

"The victim of the Lost Cause legend has been history, *for which the legend has been substituted in the national memory."*

The "Lost Cause" of the Confederacy Is a Historical Myth

Alan T. Nolan

It is often said that history is written by the victors. But according to a growing body of historians, this has not been the case with the American Civil War. Advocates of the Confederacy, including Woodrow Wilson, have hijacked history, replacing ugly truths about slavery and secession with a "Lost Cause" myth. According to this myth, the Confederacy was the noble, doomed, tragic underdog in America's most terrible conflict. This myth has proved so powerful and pervasive that most Americans, both Northerners and Southerners, have come to believe it; witness the enduring popular success of Lost Cause stories such as *Gone with the Wind*.

Historian Alan T. Nolan is the author of *Lee Considered: Robert E. Lee and Civil War History*, a book that challenges the conventional image of General Lee as a reluctant secessionist who loathed slavery. Nolan is also the coeditor of *The Myth of the Lost Cause and Civil War History*, the source of the following viewpoint. Here Nolan itemizes all the elements of Lost Cause mythology and indicts them for their pernicious effect on the nation's history.

It is fair to say that there are two independent versions of the [Civil War]. On one hand there is the *history* of the war, the account of what in fact happened. On the other there is what Gaines Foster calls the "Southern interpretation" of the event. This account, "codified" according to Foster, is generally referred to by historians today as "the Lost Cause." This version, touching almost all aspects of the struggle, originated in Southern rationalizations of the war. Then it spread to the North and became a national phenomenon. In the popular mind, the Lost Cause represents the national memory of the Civil War; it has been substituted for the *history* of the war.

The Lost Cause is therefore an American legend, an American version of great sagas like *Beowulf* and the *Song of Roland*. Generally described, the legend tells us that the war was a mawkish and essentially heroic and romantic melodrama, an honorable sectional duel, a time of martial glory on both sides, and triumphant nationalism. . . .

The victim of the Lost Cause legend has been *history*, for which the legend has been substituted in the national memory. . . .

The Lost Cause as Advocacy

The Lost Cause was expressly a rationalization, a cover-up. It is, therefore, distinctly marked by Southern advocacy. As pointed out by Michael C.C. Adams in *Our Masters the Rebels*, long before the secession crisis, Southerners "came to see themselves as representing a minority within the nation." One reason for this was "the need to justify the existence of slavery . . . even before the abolitionist attack from the North, Southerners began the defense of slavery as a social system that provided unique benefits, both for the slaves whom it placed under the fatherly care of a superior race and for the master who was given the freedom from toil necessary to the creation of a superior culture." In short, Southerners were placed in a defensive posture before the war, and this has never changed.

The advocacy aspect of the Southern legend has been express on the part of Southern spokesmen. On the back page of the April 1880 issue of the *Southern Historical Society Papers*, as well as in other issues, the following advertisement for subscriptions appears above the name of Rev. J. William Jones, D.D., secretary of the Southern Historical Society of Richmond, Virginia: "[The contents] will make our Papers interesting to all lovers of historic truth and simply INVALUABLE to those who desire to see vindicated the name and fame of those who made our great struggle for constitutional freedom." Writing whose purpose is to "vindicate" the "name and fame" of the South's "great struggle" plainly proceeds from an advocacy premise.

Douglas Southall Freeman, one of the twentieth century's most prominent historians of the war, was also quite candid regarding his concerns. In *The South to Posterity*, Freeman published a critical bibliography of works about the war. He acknowledged that he was "interested to ascertain which were the books that seemed to have made new protagonists for the South." He states that his effort is to identify the books "that have brought a new generation of Americans to understanding of the Southern point of view." Freeman clearly identified himself as an advocate, and his advocacy marked his view of the war, General [Robert E.] Lee, and other Confederate leaders. His books have been highly influential with other historians and the American public.

The Claims of the Legend

Slavery Was Not the Sectional Issue. According to the legend, slavery was not the critical issue between the sections. Slavery was trivialized as the cause of the war in favor of such things as tariff disputes, control of investment banking and the means of wealth, cultural differences, and conflict between industrial and agricultural societies. In all events, the South had *not* seceded to protect slavery!

Kenneth M. Stampp observes that Southern spokesmen "denied that slavery had anything to do with the Confederate cause," thus decontaminating it and turning it into something that they could cherish. "After Appomattox, Jefferson Davis claimed that 'slavery was in no wise the cause of the conflict' and Vice President Alexander H. Stephens argued that the war 'was not a contest between the advocates or opponents of that Peculiar Institution." The denial that slavery protection had been the genesis of the Confederacy and the purpose of secession became "a cardinal element of the Southern apologia," according to Robert F. Durden. He finds that "liberty, independence and especially states rights were advanced by countless Southern spokesmen as the hallowed principles of the Lost Cause." And James L. Roark notes that postwar Southerners manifested "a nearly universal desire to escape the ignominy attached to slavery."

The Abolitionists as Provocateurs. The status of the abolitionists in the legend is a corollary to the principle that slavery was not the cause of secession. In the context of the legend, the abolitionists' image is negative. They are seen as troublemakers and provocateurs—virtually manufacturing a disagreement between the sections that was of little or no interest to the people and had little substance.

Emancipation of the Happy Slaves

The South Would Have Given Up Slavery. Another of the assertions of the Lost Cause is that the South would have abandoned slavery of its own accord. It was simply a question of time. If the war was about slavery, it was unnecessary to the elimination of slavery because it would have died a natural death. From this premise, it is claimed that the war was foolish, a vain thing on the part of the North.

The Nature of the Slaves. Given the central role of African Americans in the sectional conflict, it is surely not surprising that Southern rationalizations have extended to characterizations of the persons of these people. In the legend there exist two prominent images of the black slaves. One is of the "faithful slave"; the other is of what William Garrett Piston calls "the happy darky stereotype." It is interesting that the faithful slave had a more or less official status in the Confederate myth. In a message to the Confederate Congress in 1863 in which he attacked the Emancipation Proclamation, President Davis called the slaves "peaceful and contented laborers." It was the uniform contention of Southern spokesmen—the press, the clergy, and the politicians—that the slaves liked their status. Fiction writers from Thomas Nelson Page, James Dixon, and Joel Chandler Harris to Walt Disney and Margaret Mitchell in our own time carried this view well into this century. In the 1930s, Hollywood's slaves were invariably happy in their slavery and affectionate toward their uniformly kind and indulgent masters. Indeed, as evidenced by the 1940 film *Santa Fe Trail*, Hollywood embraced the full range of Lost Cause stereotypes: the abolitionists, the slaves, and the valiant Southern men.

Two Peoples

The Nationalistic/Cultural Difference. Having eliminated slavery as the source of sectional contention, the South created a nationalistic/cultural basis for the disagreement. This theory was instituted on the eve of the war and became a staple of the Lost Cause during and after it. An extensive statement of the argument appeared in June 1860 in the *Southern Literary Messenger.* Northerners were said to be descended from the Anglo-Saxon tribes that had been conquered by the Norman cavaliers. The cavaliers were, of course, the ancestors of the Southerners according to this theory. It was written that the cavaliers were "descended from the Norman Barons of William the Conqueror, a race distinguished in earliest history for its warlike and fearless character, a race in all times since renowned for its gallantry, chivalry, honor, gentleness, and intellect." As described in *Why the South Lost the Civil War*, "Without its own distinctive past upon which to base its nationality, the Confederacy appropriated history and created a mythic past of exiled cavaliers and chivalrous knights."

The Military Loss

Like the apologists who created the "stabbed-in-the-back" myth to explain Germany's defeat in World War I, Lost Cause spokesmen sought to rationalize the Southern military loss. This presented a confusing and sometimes contradictory set of assertions, the first of which simply manipulated semantics: the Confederates had not really been defeated, they had instead been overwhelmed by massive Northern manpower and materiel. This was presented with a suggestion that the North's superior resources constituted Yankee trickery and unfairness. Furthermore, the

South's loss was said to be inevitable from the beginning; the fact of loss was somehow mitigated in the myth because it was said that winning had been impossible. If the Confederacy could not have won, it somehow did not lose. On the other hand, the myth asserted that had the South won at Gettysburg, it would have won the war. The loss at Gettysburg was attributed to Lt. Gen. James Longstreet. The "Longstreet-lost-it-at-Gettysburg" thesis was presented in this way by Rev. J. William Jones, secretary of the Southern Historical Society. He wrote that "the South would have won at Gettysburg, and Independence, but for the failure of *one man*" (emphasis in original).

Another Lost Cause rationale for the loss at Gettysburg was Stonewall Jackson's death earlier in 1863.

An Idealized South

The Idealized Home Front. In the context of the Lost Cause, Southern culture is portrayed as superior. William Garrett Piston finds the prewar South "blessed" in the myth, peopled by cavalier aristocrats and martyrs along with the fortunate happy darkies. Gaines Foster sees "grace and gentility" attributed to the South in the myth. The planter aristocracy, the other whites, and blacks are pictured as united in defense of the South's humane, superior culture. The "moonlight and magnolias" culture as described by Foster is fully displayed in *Gone with the Wind*, America's favorite Civil War story. That story idealized the men and women of the plantation class, suggested the superior valor of Southern manhood, and is strongly peopled with happy slaves and gentle and indulgent masters.

The Idealized Confederate Soldier. Piston writes that the Lost Cause legend "developed a romanticized stereotype of the Confederate soldier." He was invariably heroic, indefatigable, gallant, and law-abiding. It is not my intent in any way to disparage the common soldier of the Confederacy. In many ways he was the principal victim of the Lost Cause myth. Nor do I contend that the majority of Confederate soldiers believed they were fighting to preserve slavery. In fact, they were, but many of them thought in terms of defending their homeland and families and resisting what their leaders had told them was Northern aggression.

The Lawfulness of Secession. The Lost Cause doctrine endlessly asserted that secession was a constitutional right. Moreover, because it was lawful, those supporting it were not rebels or traitors; there had not been a rebellion or revolution. The premise of this contention was that because the Constitution was silent on the issue, withdrawal from the Union was permitted. It was argued that the states had entered into a compact from which they had the right to withdraw.

God-like Lee

The Saints Go Marching In. Another characteristic of the Lost Cause legend appears in its characterizations of Southern military leaders. These men, at least the successful ones, are not evaluated simply in terms of their military and leadership skills and combat effectiveness. Although they are surely given such credit, they are also presented as remarkable and saintly creatures, supermen. Generals Lee and Stonewall Jackson are the primary examples of this phenomenon. The Lee hagiography is surely well known. Douglas Southall Freeman, his leading biographer, whose treatment has been highly influential with all other Lee writers, goes to great lengths to picture Lee as Christlike. Lee's supreme, God-like status was established almost immediately after the war. As early as 1868 he was described in a Southern publication as "bathed in the white light that falls directly upon him from the smile of an approving and sustaining God." The apotheosis had advanced by 1880, when John W. Daniel, who had served on Lt. Gen. Jubal Early's staff, wrote that: "The Divinity in his bosom shown translucent through the man and his spirit rose up to the god-like." A group of twentieth-century writers including Gamaliel Bradford, Clifford Dowdey, and Freeman have carried this image of Lee well into our own time.

Saint Jackson

Stonewall Jackson is also presented as more than an effective soldier. Early Lost Cause writers like Robert Lewis Dabney and John Esten Cooke presented him as a deeply religious, mystical, eccentric, and brilliant military leader of Olympian proportions. This was also the thrust of Englishman G.F.R. Henderson's writing in

1898. The neo-Confederate writers of the Lost Cause in this century—people like James I. Robertson Jr.—are, if anything, more elaborate in their tributes to Jackson than were his early biographers. Robertson's 1997 biography describes Jackson as a "spiritual prince," "standing alone on a high pedestal," and he says that Jackson's devotion to God, duty, and country "remain treasured legacies of the American people just as they are inspirations to people everywhere." This work approvingly quotes the following tribute paid by one of Jackson's subordinate officers: "He was indeed a soldier of the cross."

National Park Service personnel conduct a tour of the grounds at Guiney Station, Virginia, including the building in which Jackson died. These affairs are in the nature of pilgrimages, with candlelight and lugubrious readings of accounts of the general's death, not unlike the reading of Christ's Passion and death on Palm Sunday at a Roman Catholic mass. . . .

The Lost Cause Legacy to History

Taken together, the elements of the Myth of the Lost Cause created the Southern image that was sought. Slavery and the slavery disagreement were excluded from that image. There had been a distinctive and superior Southern culture, benign and effective in its race relations. That culture was led by wise and superior men who seceded because they sought freedom from an oppressive Northern culture, an effort that failed because of overwhelming Northern power. The warfare itself was a contest of honor and martial glory in which the chivalrous and valorous Southerners pursued a sort of Arthurian tournament, seeking Southern independence.

The Lost Cause version of the war is a caricature, possible, among other reasons, because of the false treatment of slavery and the black people. This false treatment struck at the core of the truth of the war, unhinging cause and effect, depriving the United States of any high purpose, and removing African Americans from their true role as the issue of the war and participants in the war, and characterizing them as historically irrelevant. With slavery exorcised, it appeared that the North had conducted itself within the Union so as to provoke secession and then bloodily defeated the secessionists in war so as to compel them to stay in the Union against their will.

Slavery the Sectional Issue

The historical image of the war is, of course, quite different. It says that the seceding states were dominated by a cruel and wrongful slavery. As evidenced by the prewar political discord, the nature of the compromise efforts on the eve of Fort Sumter—all of which concerned the legal status of slavery—and the prewar statements of Southern political leaders, slavery was *the* sectional issue. Southern political leaders led their states out of the Union to protect slavery from a disapproving national majority. Although slaveholders constituted a distinct minority of Southern people, a majority of these people were committed to the institution for African Americans. The North went to war to defeat secession. The Civil War, therefore, presented three issues: (1) however flawed the circumstances, human freedom was at stake; (2) the territorial and political integrity of the United States was at stake; and (3) the survival of the democratic process—republican government of, by, and for the people—was at stake.

Secession was not therefore heroic—it was mean and narrow and a profound mistake. Its leaders were wrong and authored a major tragedy for the American people. Dismantling the United States in 1861 would not have benefited either the North or the South. On the contrary, it would have led to constant conflict over such things as access to the Mississippi River and the rights of the two nations to the territories, and it would have established the precedent that a loser in a democratic election may successfully resort to warfare, as Lincoln discussed in his Gettysburg Address. The warfare itself, in which African Americans participated in behalf of the North, was cruel and terribly destructive to the people of both sides.

"Good Faith" and Negrophobia

Confederate sympathizers today contend that the secessionists acted in good faith; this presumably means that they thought that they were doing the right thing. It would seem that this is neither here nor there in a historical sense. Leaders of all kinds of destructive causes—causes with wholly negative values—have thought they were right. It would be inflammatory to identify examples of this in modern times, but surely they occur to us. The historical question is whether, in good faith or bad, the movement that was led was positive or negative, humane or inhumane?

The Lost Cause treatment of the role of slavery in the war and its view of African Americans as subhumans not to be taken seriously formed the prelude to the myth of Reconstruction, another historical legacy of the Lost Cause. As portrayed in D.W. Griffith's *Birth of a Nation* and its updated Margaret Mitchell version, the Reconstruction myth identified the freedmen variously as shiftless fools, corrupt political connivers, or despoilers of the virtues of white women. Reconstruction was pictured as a cynical exploitation of African Americans by cynical schemers. The Ku Klux Klan existed as the shield of justice and the virtue of Southern women. This Negrophobic Reconstruction myth has been so dominant that a man as intelligent and humane as Shelby Foote commented negatively about Reconstruction in Ken Burns's Civil War television series.

The Political Legacy

The political legacy of the Lost Cause had two signal aspects. On one hand, its development facilitated the reunification of the North and South. [According to Gaines M. Foster,] ex-Confederates saw the acceptance of the myth by Northerners as "signs of respect from former foes and Northern publishers [which] made acceptance of reunion easier. By the mid-80s, most southerners had decided to build a future within a reunited nation. The North had . . . acknowledged the heroism and nobility of the Confederate effort, the honor of the South" so that "Southerners would be totally at ease in the union."

The second aspect of the political legacy concerned the status of African Americans. The virulent racism that the North shared with the South, in spite of Northern antislavery views, was a premise of the Lost Cause and the principal engine of the North's acceptance of it. The reunion was exclusively a white man's phenomenon and the price of the reunion was the sacrifice of the African Americans. Indeed, the reunion of the white race was expressly at the expense of the freedmen. The Compromise of 1877 gave the presidential election to Rutherford B. Hayes and the Republicans on the promise that Federal troops—the blacks' only shield—would be withdrawn from the South. The blacks were abandoned, the states of Confederacy were "redeemed" by the empowerment of the former Confederate political leadership, and Articles XIV (equal protection of the law) and XV (voting rights), constitutional products of the war, were permitted to atrophy for a hundred years. In short, the success of the teachings of the Lost Cause led to the nation's abandoning even its half-hearted effort to protect African Americans and bring them into the United States as equal citizens. Jim Crow, lynch law, and disfranchisement followed.

For Further Discussion

Chapter 1

1. The *Albany Atlas and Argus* was a Democratic newspaper that opposed Lincoln's election as president; the *Peoria Daily Transcript* was a Republican newspaper that endorsed Lincoln. How do you think these newspapers' political affiliations affected their editorial views on secession?

2. Both the South Carolina Convention and Abraham Lincoln rely on America's founding documents to support their viewpoints—South Carolina that secession is justified, Lincoln that it is not. Who do you think uses the founding documents more effectively in their arguments, the convention or Lincoln? Explain your response.

3. W.E.B. Du Bois was an elderly civil rights leader when he wrote this viewpoint in 1960; Thomas J. DiLorenzo is an economist who published his viewpoint in 1998. How might these differences account for their opposing opinions concerning slavery's role in starting the Civil War?

Chapter 2

1. In their viewpoints concerning the use of black soldiers by the Union, who do you think appeals more to emotion than to reason—Frederick Douglass or Garrett Davis? Explain your response.

2. Frederick Douglass was an escaped slave and abolitionist leader; Jefferson Davis was a slave owner opposed to emancipation. Despite their differences, on what points do they seem to agree about Lincoln's Emancipation Proclamation?

3. The opposing arguments of Clement L. Vallandigham and Abraham Lincoln concerning the suspension of civil liberties have been echoed during subsequent U.S. wars. When serving as commander in chief during wartime, what type of powers do you think a president should have? What type of powers do you think a president should be denied?

4. B.H. Liddell Hart portrays General William Tecumseh Sherman as a clearheaded strategist; Jack Trammell portrays him as an unbalanced and vengeful man. Which portrait do you find more convincing, and why?

Chapter 3

1. Historians agree that Lincoln might have lost the presidency if Sherman had not captured Atlanta before the 1864 election. Judging from the Democratic platform, what do you think would have been the outcome of the Civil War if Lincoln had not been reelected?
2. Historians generally believe that Robert E. Lee's decision to surrender was sensible and realistic, while Jefferson Davis's insistence on continuing a guerrilla war was irrational and deluded. Explain why you do or do not agree with them.
3. James M. McPherson argues that the Battle of Antietam marked the turning point in the Civil War, while Garry Wills argues that Lincoln's Gettysburg Address was the turning point. Choose yet another event in the Civil War and make a case for its significance in the conflict.

Chapter 4

1. There is increasing historical debate as to whether the Civil War was really a modern war. Judging from the viewpoints of Bruce Catton and Stuart L. Koehl, why do you think this debate has become so heated?
2. As a child, Woodrow Wilson witnessed the Civil War from the Southern side. Do you think Wilson's personal experience makes him more or less qualified to assess the conflict than Alan T. Nolan, who writes about the war more than a century after its occurrence? Explain your response.

✳ Chronology

1860

November 4: The antislavery Republican candidate Abraham Lincoln wins the presidency with only 40 percent of the national popular vote. He wins virtually all electoral votes in the eighteen free states but none in states south of the Mason-Dixon Line.

November 10: On receiving news of Lincoln's election, the South Carolina legislature votes to hold a special state convention to consider secession.

December 20: By a unanimous convention vote, South Carolina becomes the first state to secede from the Union. Lame-duck president James Buchanan calls secession illegal but argues that the federal government has no power to prevent it by force.

December 30–February 16: Confederate authorities seize federal arsenals and forts in South Carolina, Georgia, Florida, Louisiana, Arkansas, and Texas. One federal holdout is Fort Sumter in Charleston, South Carolina.

1861

January 9: The merchant ship *Star of the West*, sent by President Buchanan to reinforce Fort Sumter, withdraws without completing its mission after it is fired upon by South Carolina guns in Charleston Harbor.

January 9–February 18: Mississippi, Florida, Alabama, Georgia, Louisiana, and Texas secede from the Union, while Kansas is admitted as a free state. Delegates from the seven seceded states meet in Montgomery, Alabama, to form the Confederate States of America. Jefferson Davis of Mississippi is elected president, and Alexander H. Stephens of Georgia is elected vice president. Davis is inaugurated on February 18.

March 4: Abraham Lincoln is inaugurated as the sixteenth president of the United States. In his inaugural address, he denounces secession and asks the rebellious states to return peacefully to the Union. He also promises not to interfere with the institution of slavery.

March 5–April 9: President Lincoln learns that Fort Sumter is rapidly running short of supplies. He informs the governor of South Carolina that "an attempt will be made to supply Fort Sumter with provisions only." Confederate president Jefferson Davis orders Fort Sumter taken before relief arrives.

April 12–14: Confederate guns fire on Fort Sumter. The U.S. flag is hauled down and the Confederate flag raised over the fort.

April 15: President Lincoln issues a proclamation calling seventy-five thousand state militiamen into national service for ninety days. Northern states accept the call for troops; most border states reject it.

April 17: Virginia joins the Confederacy.

April 19: Lincoln orders a naval blockade of Southern ports.

April 27: Lincoln suspends the writ of habeas corpus in portions of Maryland in order to permit the military arrests of suspected secessionists in this border slave state.

May: Arkansas, Tennessee, and North Carolina join the Confederacy. The Confederacy now consists of eleven states. Twenty-three states remain in the Union, including the slave states of Delaware, Maryland, Kentucky, and Missouri.

May 13: Great Britain, the leading world power, declares neutrality in the crisis, recognizing the Confederacy as a belligerent under international law but not as an independent nation.

July 21: Confederate soldiers are victorious at the First Battle of Bull Run (or Manassas) in Virginia. Confederate general Thomas J. Jackson earns the nickname "Stonewall" for his leadership during the battle.

July 24: Lincoln places George B. McClellan in command of the main Union army of the east, called the Army of the Potomac.

August 6: Congress passes the First Confiscation Act, confiscating any property (slaves included) used directly in the Confederate war effort.

November 8: A U.S. naval ship stops a British steamer, the *Trent*, and seizes two Confederate envoys en route to England, causing a diplomatic crisis. The two envoys are released in December.

1862

February: Union forces under General Ulysses S. Grant score important victories in Tennessee by capturing Fort Henry and Fort Donelson.

March 9: The world's first battle between two ironclad ships, the Union *Monitor* and the Confederate *Virginia* (formerly the USS *Merrimack*), ends in a draw.

March 13: Congress forbids Union army officers to return fugitive slaves to their masters.

April 4: McClellan transports the Army of the Potomac to the peninsula between the York and James rivers, hoping to eventually seize the Confederate capital of Richmond. Thus begins the two-month Peninsular Campaign.

April 6–7: Grant defeats Confederate forces at the Battle of Shiloh in Tennessee. More people die in two days' fighting than in all previous wars in American history combined.

April 16: The Confederate Congress enacts the first conscription law in American history.

April 25: New Orleans, the South's largest city, surrenders to a U.S. naval force under David G. Farragut; the city is occupied by the North for the rest of the war.

June 1: Robert E. Lee takes command of the Army of Northern Virginia.

June 25–July 1: Lee attacks McClellan in the Seven Days' Battles. McClellan retreats to Harrison's Landing, his Peninsular Campaign a failure.

July 12: Lincoln meets with border state congressmen to urge compensated emancipation.

July 17: Congress passes the Second Confiscation Act, which frees all slaves whose owners are rebelling against the United States and authorizes the president to "employ" blacks for the suppression of the rebellion.

August 14: Lincoln meets with black leaders in the White House. He tells them that slavery is the "greatest wrong inflicted on any people" but also urges black colonization outside the United States.

August 29–30: The Second Battle of Bull Run (or Manassas) ends in another embarrassing defeat for the North.

September 7: The Army of Northern Virginia, under Lee, invades Maryland.

September 17: The Battle of Antietam (or Sharpsburg) in Maryland ends in about twelve thousand casualties for the North and thirteen thousand casualties for the South—the bloodiest day in American military history. Lee is compelled to withdraw to Virginia, which gives Lincoln an opportunity to take action toward emancipation.

September 22: Lincoln issues a preliminary Emancipation Proclamation, to take effect on January 1, 1863.

September 24: Lincoln suspends the writ of habeas corpus throughout the North and subjects "all persons discouraging voluntary enlistments" to martial law.

November 4: The Democrats score significant gains in the Northern congressional and state elections.

November 7: Lincoln, impatient with McClellan's failure to press his advantage following the Battle of Antietam, replaces him as commander of the Army of the Potomac with General Ambrose B. Burnside.

December 13: Burnside leads his army to a disastrous defeat at the Battle of Fredericksburg, suffering twelve thousand casualties. He is later replaced by General Joseph Hooker.

1863

January 1: The Emancipation Proclamation takes effect, freeing slaves only in areas under Confederate control. The proclamation emphasizes enlisting black soldiers for the Union cause.

March 3: Congress enacts a draft (the Enrollment Act of 1863) to raise troops. The law makes most male citizens aged twenty to forty-five liable for conscription.

May 1–4: Lee defeats a larger Union force under Hooker in the Battle of Chancellorsville. "Stonewall" Jackson is accidentally shot by one of his own men and dies on May 10.

May 5: Democratic congressman Clement L. Vallandigham is arrested and tried for treason by military authorities. He is banished to the Confederacy on May 19.

June 3: Lee leads seventy-five thousand Confederate soldiers in a campaign that will take them to Pennsylvania and culminate in the Battle of Gettysburg.

June 28: General George G. Meade replaces Hooker as commander of the Army of the Potomac.

July 1–3: The Battle of Gettysburg, Pennsylvania, leaves twenty-three thousand Confederate and twenty-eight thousand Union soldiers killed, wounded, or missing. This Union victory marks the end of the last major Confederate offensive of the war.

July 4: The town of Vicksburg, Mississippi, surrenders to Grant, ending a six-week siege. The importance of this victory ranks with that of Gettysburg.

July 13–16: Antidraft riots erupt in New York City, where mobs of poor white immigrants lynch blacks and burn buildings.

July 30: Lincoln threatens retaliation on Confederate prisoners if captured black Union soldiers are placed into slavery or otherwise mistreated by the Confederacy.

November 19: Lincoln delivers his Gettysburg Address.

1864

March 12: Grant is placed in command of all Union armies. Sherman replaces Grant as commander of western forces.

May–June: Armies of Lee and Grant clash in Virginia in the battles of the Wilderness (May 5–7), Spotsylvania Court House (May 8–19), and Cold Harbor (June 1–3). The North suffers much higher casualties than the South, but unlike previous Union generals, Grant nonetheless presses on toward Richmond.

June 7: Lincoln is renominated for president by the Republican Party. To broaden Lincoln's political base, Andrew Johnson, a Tennessee Democrat who remained loyal to the Union, is named his running mate.

June 12–18: Grant attempts to capture St. Petersburg, Virginia, south of Richmond. The attack fails, and the armies of Lee and Grant are locked into siege warfare for the next nine months.

June 15: Clement L. Vallandigham returns to Ohio from exile to denounce the Civil War as "unnecessary."

August 20: Democratic Party nominates McClellan for president. In his campaign, McClellan repudiates the Democratic Party platform, which proposes an immediate end to the war.

September 2: Northern morale rises when Union forces under Sherman capture Atlanta.

November–December: Sherman marches his army across Georgia to the Atlantic Ocean, destroying Southern economic resources and morale.

November 8: Lincoln is reelected, carrying all but three states.

1865

January 16: General Sherman issues Special Field Order 15, setting aside coastal territory in Florida, Georgia, and South Carolina for the provision of forty-acre plots for ex-slaves.

January 31: By a vote of 119-56, Congress approves the Thirteenth Amendment to the Constitution, abolishing slavery. The amendment is sent to the states for ratification.

March 4: Lincoln is inaugurated for a second term. His second inaugural address emphasizes compassion toward the South.

March 13: The Confederate Congress passes a measure authorizing enlistment of black troops, with an implied promise of freedom for slaves who serve.

April 2–3: After defeats by Grant near Petersburg, Lee evacuates Richmond, the Confederate capital.

April 9: Lee surrenders to Grant at Appomattox Court House.

April 14–15: While watching a play at Ford's Theatre in Washington, Lincoln is shot by Confederate sympathizer John Wilkes Booth. Lincoln dies the next morning. Andrew Johnson assumes the presidency.

December 13: The Thirteenth Amendment to the Constitution, abolishing slavery, is ratified by the states.

For Further Research

Historical Studies

Lerone Bennett Jr., *Forced into Glory: Abraham Lincoln's White Dream*. Chicago: Johnson, 2000.

Richard E. Beringer et al., *Why the South Lost the Civil War*. Athens: University of Georgia Press, 1986.

Ira Berlin et al., *Slaves No More: Three Essays on Emancipation and the Civil War*. New York: Cambridge University Press, 1992.

Iver Bernstein, *The New York City Draft Riots*. New York: Oxford University Press, 1990.

David W. Blight, *Race and Reunion: The Civil War in American Memory*. Cambridge, MA: Belknap, 2001.

Mark Boatner, *The Civil War Dictionary*. Rev. ed. New York: McKay, 1988.

Bruce Catton, *America Goes to War: The Civil War and Its Meaning in American Culture*. Hanover, NH: Wesleyan University Press, 1986.

———, *The Centennial History of the Civil War*. 3 vols. Garden City, NY: Doubleday, 1961–1965.

E. Merton Coulter, *The Confederate States of America, 1861–1865*. Baton Rouge: Louisiana State University Press, 1950.

Marilyn Mayer Culpepper, *Trials and Triumphs: The Women of the American Civil War*. East Lansing: Michigan State University Press, 1991.

William C. Davis, *Jefferson Davis: The Man and His Hour*. New York: HarperCollins, 1991.

William C. Davis, ed., *The Image of War, 1861–1865*. 6 vols. Garden City, NY: Doubleday, 1981–1984.

Robert F. Durden, *The Gray and the Black: The Confederate Debate on Emancipation.* Baton Rouge: Louisiana State University Press, 1972.

Paul Escott, *After Secession: Jefferson Davis and the Failure of Confederate Nationalism.* Baton Rouge: Louisiana State University Press, 1978.

Daniel Farber, *Lincoln's Constitution.* Chicago: University of Chicago Press, 2003.

Shelby Foote, *The Civil War: A Narrative.* 3 vols. New York: Random House, 1958–1974.

George M. Frederickson, *The Inner Civil War: Northern Intellectuals and the Crisis of the Union.* Urbana: University of Illinois Press, 1993.

Gary W. Gallagher and Alan T. Nolan, eds., *The Myth of the Lost Cause and Civil War History.* Bloomington: Indiana University Press, 2000.

Louis S. Gerteis, *From Contraband to Freedman: Federal Policy Toward Southern Blacks, 1861–1865.* Westport, CT: Greenwood, 1973.

William E. Gienapp, *Abraham Lincoln and Civil War America: A Biography.* New York: Oxford University Press, 2002.

Joseph T. Glatthaar, *Forged in Battle.* New York: Free Press, 1990.

Paddy Griffith, *Battle Tactics of the Civil War.* London: Yale University Press, 1989.

Hondon B. Hargrove, *Black Union Soldiers in the Civil War.* Jefferson, NC: McFarland, 1988.

B.H. Liddell Hart, *Sherman: Soldier, Realist, American.* Boston: Dodd, Mead, 1929.

Herman Hattaway and Archer Jones, *How the North Won: A Military History of the Civil War.* Urbana: University of Illinois Press, 1983.

Lee Kennett, *Sherman: A Soldier's Life.* New York: HarperCollins, 2001.

Bruce Levine, *Half Slave and Half Free: The Roots of Civil War.* New York: Hill and Wang, 1992.

Gerald Linderman, *Embattled Courage: The Experience of Combat in the American Civil War.* New York: Free Press, 1987.

Leon Litwack, *Been in the Storm So Long: The Aftermath of Slavery.* New York: Knopf, 1979.

E.B. Long, with Barbara Long, *The Civil War Day by Day: An Almanac, 1861–1865.* Garden City, NY: Doubleday, 1971.

James M. McPherson, *Battle Cry of Freedom: The Civil War Era.* New York: Oxford University Press, 1988.

———, *Crossroads of Freedom: Antietam.* New York: Oxford University Press, 2002.

———, *What They Fought For, 1861–1865.* Baton Rouge: Louisiana State University Press, 1994.

Grady McWhiney and Perry Jamieson, *Attack and Die: Civil War Military Tactics and the Southern Heritage.* Tuscaloosa: University of Alabama Press, 1982.

Allan Nevins, *Ordeal of the Union.* 4 vols. New York: Scribner, 1947.

———, *The War for the Union.* 4 vols. New York: Scribner, 1959–1971.

Alan T. Nolan, *Lee Considered: General Robert E. Lee and Civil War History.* Chapel Hill: University of North Carolina Press, 1991.

Charles Royster, *The Destructive War: William Tecumseh Sherman, Stonewall Jackson, and the Americans.* New York: Knopf, 1991.

Joel Silbey, *A Respectable Minority: The Democratic Party in the Civil War Era.* New York: W.W. Norton, 1977.

Kenneth M. Stampp, *And the War Came: The North and the Se-*

cession Crisis, 1860–1861. Baton Rouge: Louisiana State University Press, 1950.

John M. Taylor, *William Henry Seward: Lincoln's Right Hand.* New York: HarperCollins, 1991.

Hans L. Trefousse, *The Radical Republicans: Lincoln's Vanguard for Racial Justice.* New York: Knopf, 1969.

Geoffrey C. Ward, *The Civil War: An Illustrated History.* New York: Knopf, 1990.

Ronald C. White Jr., *Lincoln's Greatest Speech: The Second Inaugural Address.* New York: Simon & Schuster, 2002.

Bell Wiley, *The Life of Billy Yank.* Indianapolis: Bobbs-Merrill, 1952.

——, *The Life of Johnny Reb.* Indianapolis: Bobbs-Merrill, 1943.

T. Harry Williams, *Lincoln and His Generals.* New York: Knopf, 1952.

Garry Wills, *Lincoln at Gettysburg: The Words That Remade America.* New York: Simon & Schuster, 1992.

Bertram Wyatt-Brown, *Southern Honor: Ethics and Behavior in the Old South.* New York: Oxford University Press, 1982.

Agatha Young, *The Women and the Crisis: Women of the North in the Civil War.* New York: McDowell, Oblensky, 1959.

Document Collections and Other Primary Sources

Paul M. Angle and Earl Schenk Miers, *Tragic Years, 1860–1865: A Documentary History of the American Civil War.* New York: Simon & Schuster, 1960.

Roy P. Basler, ed., *The Collected Works of Abraham Lincoln.* New Brunswick, NJ: Rutgers University Press, 1953–1955.

Ira Berlin et al., eds., *Free at Last: A Documentary History of Slavery, Freedom, and the Civil War.* New York: New Press, 1992.

Benson Bobrick, *Testament: A Soldier's Story of the Civil War*. New York: Simon & Schuster, 2003.

Henry Steele Commager, ed., *The Blue and the Gray: The Story of the Civil War as Told by Participants*. Indianapolis: Bobbs-Merrill, 1950.

Frederick Douglass, *The Civil War, 1861–1865*. Vol. 3 of *The Life and Writings of Frederick Douglass*, ed. Philip S. Foner. New York: International, 1952.

Clifford Dowdey and Louis H. Manarin, eds., *The Wartime Papers of R.E. Lee*. Boston: Little, Brown, 1961.

William W. Freeling and Craig M. Simpson, eds., *Secession Debated: Georgia's Showdown in 1860*. New York: Oxford University Press, 1992.

Ulysses S. Grant, *Memoirs and Selected Letters: Personal Memoirs of U.S. Grant, Selected Letters 1839–1865*. New York: Library of America, 1990.

Richard B. Harwell, ed., *The Civil War Reader*. New York: Mallard Press, 1991.

Harold Holzer, ed., *The Lincoln-Douglas Debates*. New York: HarperCollins, 1993.

Louis P. Masur, ed., *"The Real War Will Never Get in the Books": Selections from Writers During the Civil War*. New York: Oxford University Press, 1993.

Paul F. Paskoff and Daniel J. Wilson, eds., *The Cause of the South: Selections from De Bow's Review, 1846–1867*. Baton Rouge: Louisiana State University Press, 1982.

Howard C. Perkins, ed., *Northern Editorials on Secession*. Gloucester, MA: Peter Smith, 1964.

James D. Richardson, ed., *The Messages and Papers of Jefferson Davis and the Confederacy*. New York: Chelsea House, 1966.

William Tecumseh Sherman, *The Memoirs of General William T.*

Sherman by Himself. Bloomington: Indiana University Press, 1957.

George W. Smith and Charles Judah, eds., *Life in the North During the Civil War.* Albuquerque: University of New Mexico Press, 1966.

Kenneth M. Stampp, ed., *The Causes of the Civil War.* Rev. ed. New York: Simon & Schuster, 1974.

C. Vann Woodward, ed., *Mary Chestnut's Civil War.* New Haven, CT: Yale University Press, 1981.

Web Sites

The Civil War, www.civilwar.com/homemain.htm. This Web site contains a time line, government documents, letters, diaries, music, information on battles and places, and links to other sites. It also includes a discussion board and a bookstore.

The Civil War, www.pbs.org/civilwar. This is the companion site for the 1990 PBS documentary created by Ken Burns. In addition to a rich collection of images and information about the war, the site includes classroom materials and lesson plans. It also features information about the making of Burns's celebrated documentary.

The Civil War Home Page, www.civil-war.net. This Web site contains thousands of pages of Civil War material, including photographs, official records, census information, and links to other sites. It also features message boards with lively online discussions of the war, its causes, and its battles.

The Collected Works of Abraham Lincoln, www.hti.umich.edu/l/lincoln. Roy P. Basler's multivolume *The Collected Works of Abraham Lincoln* of 1953 remains the standard primary source for Lincoln's thought and writings. This Web site makes Basler's entire collection available in electronic form, offering a variety of search options.

✲ Index